THE GORILLA

Look for these and other books in the
Lucent Endangered Animals and Habitats Series:

The Amazon Rain Forest
The Bald Eagle
The Bear
The Elephant
The Giant Panda
The Gorilla
The Manatee
The Oceans
The Rhinoceros
Seals and Sea Lions
The Shark
The Tiger
The Whale
The Wolf

Other related titles in the Lucent Overview Series:

Acid Rain
Endangered Species
Energy Alternatives
Garbage
The Greenhouse Effect
Hazardous Waste
Ocean Pollution
Oil Spills
Ozone
Pesticides
Population
Rainforests
Recycling
Saving the American Wilderness
Vanishing Wetlands
Zoos

THE GORILLA

BY ANNE AKE

Endangered Animals & Habitats

LUCENT BOOKS, INC.
SAN DIEGO, CALIFORNIA

Library of Congress Cataloging-in-Publication Data

Ake, Anne, 1943–
 The gorilla / by Anne Ake.
   p.   cm. — (Endangered animals & habitats)
 Includes bibliographical references (p.   ) and index.
 Summary: Discusses the physical characteristics, behavior,
habitats, and endangered status of the gorilla.
 ISBN 1-56006-492-7 (lib. bdg. : alk. paper)
 1. Gorilla—Juvenile literature.   2. Endangered species—
Juvenile literature.   [1. Gorilla.   2. Endangered species.]
I. Title.   II. Series.
QL737.P96A35   1999
599.884—dc21   98-53231
                                                              CIP
                                                               AC

Copyright © 1999 by Lucent Books, Inc.
P.O. Box 289011, San Diego, CA 92198-9011
Printed in the U.S.A.

Contents

Introduction

When I look back on my time with the gorillas, I remember the magic of the animals, the beauty of a family patriarch, his silver saddle sparkling like morning frost. Such images are anchored in my heart. That in this supposedly enlightened age the mountain gorilla remains so vulnerable, its existence so wholly dependent on human whim, fills me with exasperation and indignation. Its loss would be a death in the family.

—George B. Schaller, *Gorilla*

FOR THOUSANDS OF YEARS gorillas have lived peacefully on the misted slopes of the Virunga Volcanoes and in the steamy lowland jungles of Africa, but they have been known to the Western world for only a little more than one hundred years. In that time, contact with humans has brought the gorilla to near extinction. Approximately six hundred mountain gorillas remain in the world. Although lowland gorillas still number in the thousands, they are seriously threatened, and their numbers are dropping.

The relationship between humans and gorillas began badly. Gorillas are large, hairy, and rather frightening in appearance. It is easy to imagine that they are dangerous and ferocious. Gorillas are, in fact, very powerful animals and can be formidable foes when cornered, but they are generally peace-loving and nonaggressive. Humans saw their huge size and heard their defensive roar and did not recognize their peaceable nature. Not surprisingly, most of the early contacts between gorillas and humans ended with gorillas being killed.

A captive male lowland gorilla strikes a pensive pose. Gorillas face extinction as a result of increased human contact.

In 1856 Paul du Chaillu was the first white man to shoot and kill a gorilla. He wrote exaggerated stories about the ferocity of the huge apes:

> Nearly six feet high (he proved two inches shorter), with immense body, huge chest, and great muscular arms, with fierce glaring large deep gray eyes, and a hellish expression of face, which seemed like some nightmare vision: thus stood before us, this king of the African forests.

> He was not afraid of us. He stood there, and beat his breast with his huge fists till it resounded like an immense bass drum, which is their mode of offering defiance; meantime giving vent to roar after roar . . . we fired and killed him.[1]

It is easy to see how adventurers like Du Chaillu came to see the gorilla as a savage and defiant beast. Descriptions such as this contributed to the popularity of gorilla heads and hands as trophies among hunters and souvenir seekers.

The search for scientific knowledge

Gorillas were not only prized by trophy hunters, but also killed in the name of scientific study. In 1902 Captain Oscar von Beringe was responsible for identifying the mountain gorilla as a separate species. He accomplished this by killing two of them and sending their skeletons to a German anatomist for study. Naturalist Carl Akeley killed five mountain gorillas in 1921 to preserve them for the American Museum of Natural History. Akeley was so taken with the huge primates that he became one of the first people to feel concern for their future. He began work to convince the Belgian government, at the time the colonial power over wide ranges of gorilla habitat, to establish a park for their protection. Because of his efforts, Africa's first national park, Albert National Park, was opened in 1925. Akeley returned to Africa in 1926 for the purpose of studying the gorillas without killing them. He died early in the expedition and was buried in a meadow in the park he helped create.

Following Akeley's death, almost forty years passed before humans began to gain any real understanding of the gorilla. George Schaller began the first scientific field study of mountain gorilla behavior in 1959. At around the same time Jane Goodall began her landmark study of chimpanzees. In the years to follow, fellow field researchers began major studies of the other great apes, the bonobo and the orangutan. Across the world from the free-living apes, studies of captive apes focused on intelligence, problem solving, and language abilities. Humankind's understanding of the great apes began to take shape.

As part of his study Schaller took a census of the mountain gorilla population and learned that they were already at the brink of extinction. At that time there were fewer

A hunter and his spear-carrying guides pose beside their towering trophy in this 1935 photograph.

than six hundred mountain gorillas in existence. It was clear to conservationists that without some intervention on their behalf the mountain gorilla would soon vanish from the earth. What began as a quest for knowledge turned into a fight against time to save our nearest relatives.

A dubious future

Human activities such as hunting and farming continue to take a deadly toll on gorillas and the other great apes, directly and indirectly. Desperate human needs resulting from overpopulation, civil war, poverty, and famine draw attention and funds away from the plight of the gorilla. The search for ways to reconcile the needs of humans and gorillas grows in importance as we learn more about the evolutionary relationships between primates. Following a 1991 return trip to the site of his early gorilla study, George Schaller wrote:

> The gorilla, of course, is more than an animal. These apes are a primal part of human heritage. Our kin. We traveled down different evolutionary paths, the gorillas creating their own world, complete and coherent, and humans shaping theirs. No one who looks into a gorilla's eyes—intelligent, gentle, vulnerable—can remain unchanged, for the gap between ape and human vanishes; we know that the gorilla still lives within us. Do gorillas also recognize this ancient connection? [2]

1

The Gorilla: The Largest Primate

He lay on the slope, propped on his huge shaggy arms, and the muscles of his broad shoulders and silver back rippled. He gave an impression of dignity and restrained power, of absolute certainty in his majestic appearance.

—George B. Schaller, *Gorilla*

GORILLAS HAVE CAPTURED humans' imagination since early hunters returning from safaris in Africa told exciting tales of facing the savage beasts. These exaggerated tales built a legacy of fear and misinformation. Because so few facts were available about free-living gorillas, believing in the frightening image painted by these travelers was easy. We now know that although gorillas will defend themselves and their group, they will retreat when possible and are highly unlikely to initiate an attack.

George Schaller traveled to the mountains of central Africa in 1959 to spend more than a year studying the mountain gorilla. He made daily trips into the forests to observe gorillas in their natural habitat. He went alone and unarmed and presented no threat to the gorillas. He was able to observe gorillas going about their daily routines rather than responding to a threat. Instead of the savage beasts he had been led to expect, he found family groups of gentle, peace-loving animals. In an article for *National Geographic* magazine Schaller wrote:

My task was not to capture or master them but solely to interpret their life. So I approached them with empathy and respect, wanting nothing from them but peace and proximity. And they accepted my presence with an astounding generosity of spirit.[3]

Through carefully documented observations Schaller began to compile data on the natural history, social structure, and environmental requirements of the gorilla. He learned that the gorilla is neither savage beast nor lovable teddy bear but a complex animal with a unique social structure and code of etiquette. Schaller was followed in 1967 by Dian Fossey, who continued her field research and advocacy of the gorillas until her death in 1985. Like Schaller, Fossey found gorillas to be gentle creatures of a complexity much greater than she had expected. To ingratiate herself among her study population, Fossey learned to imitate their knuckle walk, hooting noises, and social be-

Koko, a captive female lowland gorilla, uses sign language to communicate with Dr. Francine Patterson (left) and another researcher.

haviors. In time the gorillas lost their fear of her and allowed her to observe their life at close range. At times they allowed or initiated physical contact and picked up and examined her camera and other gear. Most of what we know about the natural history of the gorilla comes from the work of Schaller and Fossey.

While Fossey worked in the field, the connections between ape and human were also being explored by researchers working with captive gorillas. The most well known of these captive gorillas is Koko, a female lowland gorilla studied by Dr. Francine Patterson of the Gorilla Foundation. Koko cuddles a pet cat and uses sign language to communicate with Patterson and other researchers. Through both field studies and work with captive gorillas, scientists are learning that the gap between humans and the other primates is not nearly as wide as they once believed.

Primates

Nearly two hundred animals are classified as primates, including humans, apes, monkeys, marmosets, tamarins, and lemurs. To understand the gorilla, it is necessary to understand something about this extended evolutionary family. The term *primate* refers to a group of animals adapted to living in trees. Primates are a very diverse group that became masters of the trees because of some special traits that give them an advantage over other climbing animals.

Almost all primates have hands with five digits including an opposable thumb, which gives them the ability to grab and hold onto a tree limb. Most also have sensitive finger pads and flat fingernails instead of claws. Grasping a limb makes climbing easier and reduces the risk of falling. It also gives primates a size advantage over other tree dwellers. They can grow much larger than other climbing animals and still support their weight with a firm grasp. A few other large mammals, such as cougars and bears, sometimes climb trees, but they cannot climb with the speed and agility of the primates.

Primates also have very good vision. They rely on their eyes rather than their noses to search for food and to detect

A mountain gorilla uses his opposable thumb to grasp a stick.

enemies. Not only can primates see well, but they can see in three dimensions. Most mammals' eyes are positioned at the sides of the head, like those of rabbits or horses. The left eye and the right eye see different segments of the landscape. Primates' eyes are close together facing nearly the same direction. The area seen by the right eye overlaps that seen by the left eye. Overlapping fields of vision make it possible to see in three dimensions. Three-dimensional viewing is important for judging distances accurately. Many primates travel by jumping from limb to limb. Their improved vision helps them judge the distance to the next limb.

A third characteristic of most primates is a large brain. Primates come in all sizes, but their brains are generally larger than the brains of other animals of similar size. They are intelligent and learn new skills quickly. The apes and humans have the most highly developed brains of all the primates. Many similarities exist between the brains of

A young gorilla gazes into a photographer's camera lens. Overlapping fields of visions enable gorillas to have three-dimensional sight.

apes and humans, but human brains are more highly developed in the areas of abstract thought, speech, and language abilities.

Advanced primates

Primates are divided into two groups—prosimians, or primitive primates, and anthropoids. Lemurs, bush babies, tarsiers, and potros are all prosimians. Monkeys and apes are classified as anthropoids. Monkeys, the first of the anthropoids to evolve, are more highly developed than the primitive primates, but less so than the apes or humans. One important difference between anthropoids and the primitive primates can be seen in their hands and feet. Primitive primates can grasp, but all of their fingers open and close as a unit. Anthropoids can move their fingers and toes individually. This enables them to pick up and manipulate small objects.

The great apes and humans are both members of the hominoid family within the anthropoid group. They are more highly developed than the other anthropoids. The great apes include gorillas, chimpanzees, orangutans, and bonobos. Their brains are even larger and better developed than the monkeys, and they have better use of their hands and improved eye-hand coordination.

At some point in the evolutionary process humankind climbed out of the trees to become the dominant life form on earth. Humans can use tools, think in abstract terms, and learn a language, and they can have and express emotions. Until recent years humans believed that these traits were theirs alone. They thought that these traits set humans apart from all other animals.

Studies of the great apes have changed scientists' way of thinking. Although these special traits may be much more highly developed in humans, they have all been observed in the great apes. Scientists such as George Schaller, Dian Fossey, Francine Patterson, and Jane Goodall have shown that apes can use tools, can communicate with each other and humans through a form of language, and can have and express emotions.

Mountain Gorilla: Best Known, Least Seen

We know more about mountain gorillas than any other group, but few people have ever seen one. There are no mountain gorillas in captivity. Almost all captive gorillas are of the western lowland species.

Why is this true? Researchers have found it easier to study mountain gorillas. Even though they live high in the mountains, their habitat is more accessible. Lowland gorillas wander farther, spend more time in the trees, and live in areas where the jungle foliage is thicker, all of which makes it more difficult for researchers to observe families over a long period of time, so most long-term studies feature mountain gorillas.

Lowland gorillas, especially western lowland, adapt better to life in captivity. Today no mountain gorillas and only a very few eastern lowland gorillas live in captivity. It is now illegal to capture and export wild gorillas.

Gorilla hands bear a strong resemblance to human hands and should be well suited to tool use. Their grasp is precise; a gorilla can pick up a single grape without crushing it. However, unlike chimpanzees, gorillas have not been observed using tools in the wild. This potential may be undeveloped because their vegetarian diet is easily accessible without tools. Captive gorillas have been taught to use tools, including, on occasion, computers.

All of the great ape species have been involved in language studies and have demonstrated substantial ability to communicate with humans. Francine Patterson of the Gorilla Foundation has studied language ability with the gorillas Koko and Michael for many years. The apes communicate with humans through sign language, symbol boards, and computers. Koko has a vocabulary of more than one thousand words, and has demonstrated the ability to express abstract ideas. However, this ability in apes seems to be rudimentary; language ability and abstract thought processes are still the most distinct differences between human and ape. George Schaller has described apes as being at the dawn of abstract and conceptual thought.

Gorilla anatomy

The gorilla is the largest living primate. Males weigh from three hundred to five hundred pounds. A male in his normal stance, with back feet and front knuckles on the ground, is about four and a half feet tall, but at his full erect height he may be close to six feet tall. Females are smaller and usually weigh between one hundred fifty and two hundred fifty pounds; their erect height is approximately five feet. Gorillas walk on all fours—on the soles of their feet and the knuckles of their hands—although they will often stand erect, especially when they feel threatened.

Gorillas have short sturdy legs and long powerful arms. A male gorilla's armspan can reach nine feet. Much gorilla mass is muscle, so they are very strong for their size. Powerful neck

Gorilla Sizes and Weights

	height (standing)	arm span	weight
Mountain Gorilla (Gorilla gorilla beringei)	5 ft. 8 in.	7 ft. 6 in.	343 lbs.
Western Lowland Gorilla (Gorilla gorilla gorilla)	5 ft. 6 in.	7 ft. 8 in.	307 lbs.
Eastern Lowland Gorilla (Gorilla gorilla graueri)	5 ft. 9 in.	8 ft. 6 in.	360 lbs.

All statistics are for mature male gorillas. Mature females are approximately half the weight of males. Infant gorillas weigh about 5 lbs. at birth.

muscles make their large heads appear cone-shaped. Black or brownish-gray fur covers the gorilla's black skin. Some gorillas have reddish hair on their heads, and males develop a saddle of silver hair across their back as they age. The dominant male in a family is called the silverback, and immature males are called blackbacks.

George Schaller describes his impression of the first gorillas he saw when he arrived in Africa: "Their hair was not merely black, but a shining blue-black, and their black faces shone as if polished. The large male . . . was the most magnificent animal I had ever seen."[4]

Habitat

All wild gorillas live in Africa. At least three subspecies, or races, of gorillas live in different parts of central and western Africa: the mountain gorilla, the western lowland gorilla, and the eastern lowland gorilla. Some scientists believe that isolated populations may actually represent new, as yet unidentified subspecies. The differences between the subspecies are slight, and result primarily from adaptations to the environment. For instance, mountain gorillas have longer body hair to compensate for the cooler mountain climate. The mountain gorilla also has more expanded nostrils and a broader chest, perhaps an adaptation to the thin mountain air.

All subspecies of gorillas, in fact all apes, are threatened or endangered. Most seriously endangered is the mountain gorilla. Less than six hundred remain in the wild; there are none in captivity. They live in an area of approximately 285 square miles in the Bwindi Impenetrable Forest and the Virunga Volcanoes, a chain of eight extinct or dormant volcanos in the center of Africa where the borders of Uganda, Rwanda, and the Democratic Republic of the Congo (DRC) meet. No one knows for sure how many western lowland gorillas remain in the wild. Most scientists estimate that there are between 10,000 and 35,000, but some believe there are as many as one hundred thousand. There are approximately 550 in captivity worldwide. In the wild, they can be found in the forests of Cameroon, Congo, Nigeria, Central African Republic, and DRC. Approximately 4,000

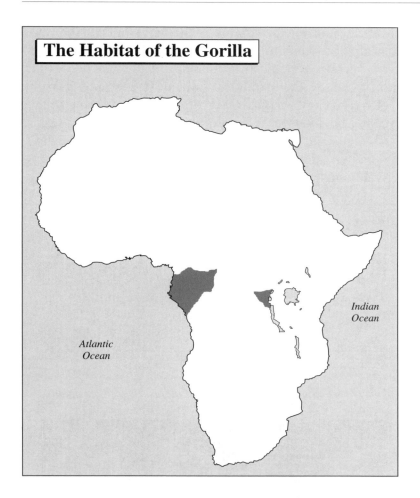

The Habitat of the Gorilla

Atlantic Ocean

Indian Ocean

eastern lowland gorillas live in eastern DRC. There are only four known to be in captivity. Although the mountain gorilla is currently the most seriously endangered, all three races face the pressures of declining habitat and poaching.

Diet

Gorillas eat more than two hundred different kinds of leaves, fruit, tubers, fungi, and flowers that grow in the African forests. Favorite foods include wild celery, thistles, bamboo, and bracket fungus, a hard shelflike fungus that grows on the trunks of trees. They occasionally stray from their vegetarian diet and eat termites or other insects. Unlike their relatives the chimpanzees, they do not hunt and eat meat. Gorillas have large potbellied stomachs because the large amounts of foliage they eat distend their stomachs. Males eat about fifty pounds a day. They get all the moisture they need from the foliage. It was once thought that free-living gorillas never drank water, but they have recently been observed both drinking and playing in water. In undisturbed habitat, food is plentiful and the gorilla's life centers around seeking choice foods and establishing social bonds within the family group.

Snowflake

Most gorillas are very dark in color, but Snowflake, a male gorilla who lives at the Barcelona Zoo, is white. Snowflake is not an albino, but a true white gorilla. There is only one white gorilla in captivity, and only one other has been sighted in the wild.

Zoo officials found a mate for Snowflake in hopes that he would sire a whole line of white gorillas. So far their offspring have all been black like their mother.

Snowflake, a rare white gorilla, lounges in his enclosure in Spain's Barcelona Zoo.

Breeding

Male gorillas become sexually mature at eleven to thirteen years of age, females a year or so earlier. The dominant silverback in a family group has exclusive breeding rights to the primary females in his group. He may allow young silverbacks to breed with females who are his daughters or of low rank within the group. Inbreeding within family groups is common. However, the social shuffling of the group assures some genetic diversity. Young males often leave the group when they reach sexual maturity. They join bachelor colonies until they can get females of their own. Sometimes they acquire females through violent altercations with established groups, but more often conflict is a lot of bluff and bluster with little physical contact. Females sometimes leave their group when the only male available for breeding is their father. They may join an existing family, or pair up with a young bachelor to start a new group.

A mountain gorilla munches on bamboo and other foliage in the Virunga Mountains of Rwanda. Male gorillas eat nearly fifty pounds of vegetation each day.

Gorillas have a slow rate of reproduction. Females do not give birth for the first time until they are about ten years old. Males are usually between twelve and fifteen years old before they become sexually active. The gestation period for gorillas is approximately eight and a half months. Females typically give birth to one infant every three to four years, and 40 to 60 percent of gorilla infants die in their first year of life from disease, injury, or infanticide. The low reproductive rate makes the loss of even a single individual significant to these highly endangered animals.

Gorilla infants

Newborn gorillas are tiny and helpless. They weigh about three to four pounds and have very little hair except for a bit of fuzz on top of their heads. For the first couple of months they travel safely clinging to the hair of their mother's chest. As they mature they crawl around and ride on her back. By five or six months the gorilla youngster ventures out of its mother's lap occasionally to explore the world around it.

Gorilla mothers keep a close eye on their infants as they begin to test their independence. Should the infant venture a bit too far, its white tail tuft is easy to spot in the jungle. As the youngster grows, it begins to seek out other juveniles for games and play fighting.

Gorillas tend to their infants with affection, playfulness, and patience. Mothers and other group members, including the silverback, teach the youngsters all they need to know about social and sexual behavior, what to eat, and how to build nests. Infants are nursed and carried around by their mothers until they are weaned at three to four years of age. When the mother gives birth again, the older sibling, especially if it is a female, helps to care for and teach the new infant. Rowdy youngsters are disciplined with stern looks and piglike grunts. Most young gorillas maintain a close relationship with their mother even after they leave her nest and become independent members of the group. Many, especially females, will remain with the group for life.

Much like human parents, gorillas shower their young with affection and attention.

Silverbacks treat their youngsters with tolerance and affection; however, they have been known to kill the offspring of newly acquired females. Scientists speculate that the silverback eliminates the infant he did not sire in order to be able to breed with the new female sooner. Otherwise he might have to wait three or four years until she weans her infant and comes into estrus (is ready to mate) again.

Social life

Gorillas live in family groups of from three to thirty individuals. The silverback leader is sometimes supported by a second silverback, usually one of his sons. There may be one or two younger males, or blackbacks; several females; a few juveniles; and infants. Except for some exchange of young adults with other groups, family groups form strong bonds and stay together for many years. Gorillas live for approximately thirty-five years in the wild and many spend all or most of their life within one group.

Gorillas are gentle, intelligent animals. They smile, chuckle, purr, and sometimes shed tears. They often recognize several generations of kin and form long-lasting relationships with other individuals. They appear to feel and express grief. Jeffrey Masson reports in his book *When Elephants Weep:*

> When Marchessa, an elderly female mountain gorilla, died, the silverback male of her group became subdued and was heard to whimper frequently, the only time such a sound had been heard from a silverback. These two wild gorillas may have spent as much as thirty years of their lives together. [6]

Gorillas live in family groups consisting of three to thirty individuals and often form lifelong bonds with other family members.

Gorilla families form close ties, but with a well-established pecking order. Pecking order refers to the ranking system of animals in a group. The silverback is the highest-ranked

A Different Wrinkle

Gorillas recognize each other by facial features, body shape, and size. Until they know a group well, it is hard for researchers to tell one gorilla from another. Gorillas can be identified by their nose print just as humans can be identified by fingerprints. The wrinkles around a gorilla's nose are different on every gorilla. Researchers make sketches and photographs of this distinctive feature to help them identify individuals within a group.

gorilla in a group and his relationship with other members helps establish their position in the group. Usually the first females acquired by the silverback have the most status. Their young will also have more status than the young of lower-ranking females.

Sometimes members of the group bicker among themselves, but usually without genuine aggression. They express their feelings through pig grunts, facial expressions, shoving, and biting. These altercations between group members seldom result in injury.

A gorilla's day

On a typical day the group will wake up between six and eight A.M. and begin its search for food. Food is usually plentiful, so they can choose among favorites. Sometimes they take time to peel fruit or strip the outer bark from stalks. During the day, they may travel only a few hundred feet or more than a mile. The silverback chooses the route and sets the pace. He may slow the pace of the entire group for the sake of a sick or elderly member.

Around ten A.M. it is time to play, groom each other, and nap. Each member of the group uses twigs, small branches, and leaves to build a simple day nest for a nap. Each adult gorilla builds its own nest.

In the afternoon the group will continue on its way. Foraging as they go, they will travel until around five o'clock. At the end of the day, group members spend some time

Two mountain gorillas enjoy an afternoon nap in the soft foliage of their nest.

grooming each other and playing with the young ones before preparing night nests. Night nests are sturdier and more elaborate than day nests. Foliage is bent and formed into a bathtub-shaped resting place. Infants sleep with their mothers until they are about three or four years old. Gorillas sleep about thirteen hours out of every twenty-four.

Sometimes nests are built in trees, but are more often on the ground. Comfort, rather than camouflage or defense, is the main goal in nest building, since gorillas have no significant natural enemies other than man.

Defense

Only a minimal amount of effort must be devoted to defending the group from natural enemies in the forest. Violence is unusual, even between rival groups. Intruders, whether they are rival silverbacks or prowling leopards, are met with a show of force by the silverback. He stands upright to show off his full size and pounds his chest with cupped hands making a pok-a-pok-pok sound. He may roar, wave his arms, and tear up nearby brush to frighten off the intruder. Sometimes he nonchalantly pretends to nibble on a few leaves to show his lack of concern. Usually the intruder retreats when faced by this huge, ferocious-sounding beast. The silverback then returns to foraging and watching over his family.

Occasionally, a show of force is not enough. Sometimes there are violent battles between rival groups. The group will also attempt to fight off poachers if a group member has been caught in a snare or captured. The silverback, and other members of the group, will fight to the death to defend an infant. This fierce family loyalty has contributed to the endangered status of the species. Poachers have wiped out entire families to steal one infant gorilla.

A male gorilla displays his teeth in an attempt to intimidate an intruder.

The largest primate has often been misunderstood. While his nature and environmental needs remained hidden in the deep jungle he was defined by the biases of humankind. It was not until twentieth-century field biologists such as Schaller and Fossey began to delve into gorilla behavior that the ape's true nature began to be exposed. Today a large body of research data documents the natural history of our close evolutionary kin, the gorilla. Yet these endangered beings are far from being fully understood.

2

Deforestation
and War

You can hear the rage of saws upon my friends, the big trees.
They are cutting this paradise.

—Giuseppe Vassallo

AFRICA IS A VAST CONTINENT of great beauty and diversity, comprising one-fifth of the land surface of the earth. Within its area are many widely different ecosystems, including deserts, mountains, grasslands, wetlands, and jungles. It is home to many plant and animal species found no other place on earth. Many of them are endangered or threatened. Others are already extinct.

Archaeologists believe that many higher primates, including man, evolved here. At least sixty-four species of primates still live in Africa. Of these, the human species is the only one not declining in numbers. The human population of Africa numbers more than a half-billion today and is increasing faster than anywhere else on earth. Much of this rapidly growing population suffers from poverty, drought, famine, and disease.

The conflicting needs of humans and wildlife are pulling Africa in many directions. The large number of people without adequate food and shelter puts a severe strain on the environment. The outside world's hunger for Africa's great wealth of natural resources causes even greater strain. Natural habitats quickly disappear under the pressure to fill these human needs. The rainforest, vital habitat for gorillas and other wildlife, is shrinking. The great apes are being pushed to the brink of extinction by the desperate needs of a growing human population.

Where gorillas live

Most people associate Africa with images of dense jungle. Jungle is a word used to describe several types of dense tropical forest, especially secondary rainforest. Secondary rainforest has more undergrowth than primary rainforest and forms lush habitat for wildlife. This type of forest once covered most of west-central Africa. It is prime gorilla habitat. Gorillas spend most of their time on the ground rather than in the treetops, and the thick underbrush of secondary forests provides ample food, shelter, and nesting materials.

For thousands of years the forest provided for the needs of the wildlife and the forest people without suffering any harmful effects. Since World War II conditions have changed dramatically. New technology brought more efficient harvesting, farming, and mining techniques, and Africa discovered a worldwide market for the rich resources of her forests. Reaping the benefits of world progress seemed like a smart thing to do. Africa desperately needed the income, and the forest seemed almost limitless. More than 45 percent of forest cover in Africa has since been lost and 95 percent of the remainder is vulnerable to commercial interests.

Eucalyptus trees are harvested on a South African plantation. As the jungles of Africa give way to human encroachment, gorillas face habitat loss and a growing threat of extinction.

What has happened to the forest?

A variety of forces are attacking the forest ecosystems of Africa. Foreign corporations are leaders in the destruction. The beautiful hardwoods are in demand by foreign markets for the manufacture of furniture and accessories. Lesser

Rainforests and the Weather

Scientists are just beginning to understand that the world's rainforests have a global importance that goes well beyond providing habitat for plants and animals. They affect the weather and climate. Rainforests provide a high percentage of the world's water catchment area. Without the forests to store water, streams would disappear during the dry season and deprive the human population of water. This is happening in some areas of Africa.

The rainforests also absorb large quantities of solar radiation. Without the forests, more of the sun's radiation is bounced back from the surface. This can result in changes in wind currents, disruption in convection patterns, and rainfall in parts of the world far from the tropics.

Thousands of acres of forest are cleared every year by burning. Carbon dioxide released from burning forests is helping to increase the so-called greenhouse effect. The greenhouse effect causes drier, hotter climates in many areas of the earth.

woods are popular for crates, plywood, and products made from wood chips. Trees are also cut to make charcoal. Some charcoal is shipped to foreign markets and some is used to power industrial plants within Africa. Charcoal production not only destroys trees and wildlife, but creates a pall of smoke that affects air quality hundreds of miles away.

Technological advances have made the harvesting of the forest faster, easier, and often more destructive. The forest falls quickly under the assault of heavy equipment brought in by giant corporations. African governments are caught between the promise of foreign money and the desire to protect their natural resources. In countries burdened by debt and in need of cash to solve immediate people problems, the decision is often inevitable: the money wins.

Harvesting the trees is not the only reason for clearing the forest. Land is cleared for agricultural use as well. The growing African population needs more and more land for raising crops and cattle. Native farmers are often disappointed when they clear a parcel of land. Rainforests are rich and lush, but their growing requirements are very different from those of crops or pastures. The cleared soil is poor and unproductive. The thin layer of topsoil soon washes away, leaving barren red earth. Again, foreign corporations have the advantage. They can provide the chemical fertilizers and irrigation needed to make the land productive. They produce valuable crops such as coffee, but little of the profit stays in Africa to aid the local economy.

The same soil that produces lush forest is also rich in rare minerals and precious metals. Mining these resources

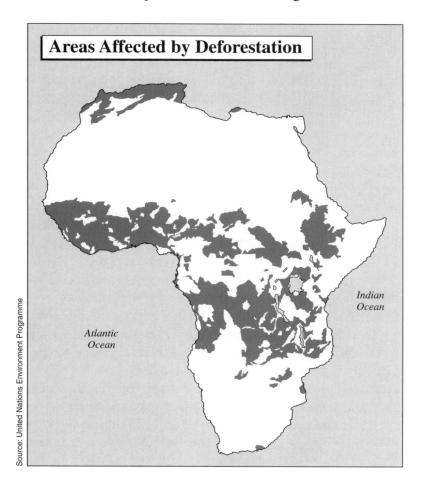

Areas Affected by Deforestation

Indian Ocean

Atlantic Ocean

Source: United Nations Environment Programme

The disrupted soil from a Rwandan gold mine contrasts with the pristine landscape of the remaining rainforest.

provides another reason for cutting trees. Miners operate deep in the forest where they fell trees, dig deep pits, and dump highly toxic chemicals used in the mining process into the ground or streams. Land for mines and agriculture is often cleared by burning, adding to the smoke of charcoal production. In fact, more rainforest is lost to burning than to any other method.

How deforestation affects gorillas

Relentless deforestation is taking its toll on the gorilla population. Once, gorillas lived deep in the forest where they were seldom seen except by native tribesmen. Now the forest is shrinking, and timber companies are cutting roads that reach deep into the remaining forest, leaving the gorillas exposed and vulnerable. They are easy prey for poachers and are sometimes killed by farmers as well. Small areas of forest surrounded by cultivated fields tempt gorillas to venture out of the woods to feed on tender young shoots in the fields. Human food is in short supply and the farmers feel justified in killing gorillas to protect their crops.

Many gorillas now live in areas that have been set aside as national parks, but even these lands are not well protected. Economic pressures have caused governments to decrease the size of the parks and to open parklands for clearing. In a 1995 article for *National Geographic,* George Schaller writes about the release of parklands in the Virunga mountains for farming and logging operations in the 1950s and 1960s. "It was a desolate time, to which the gorillas could be only mute and passive witnesses."[7] Conservation groups fight to maintain existing parklands and to have additional tracts protected, but cash-starved governments continue to give in to the offers of foreign enterprise.

Gorillas are being forced into small islands of forest. Their naturally nomadic lifestyle is altered and they are cut off from contact with other gorilla groups. Laura Spinney, a writer for *New Scientist,* says, "By building roads and opening up the forests, the companies make it easier for hunters to get to the wildlife and transport carcasses back to towns, often using the loggers' lorries [trucks] and boats. Roads and logging also cause fragmentation of wildlife habitats."[8]

The long-term effects on gorillas left isolated in small areas of fragmented forest are not yet clear, but disruption of their normal range and feeding patterns are apparent. When gorilla groups are cut off from one another they cannot exchange young, sexually mature members with other groups. This limits the genetic diversity needed to maintain a strong healthy population.

John Robinson of the Wildlife Conservation Society believes that even if populations dropped to "as little as one percent of their original levels, they can survive as long as the forest is unbroken. As soon as it is fragmented, species are prevented from recolonizing areas that have been emptied."[9]

In some areas, already weakened gorilla populations have suffered from mysterious illnesses. In a 1996 *New York Times* article Howard W. French reports:

A sprawling tea farm cuts into Rwanda's tropical Nyungwe Forest, decreasing the habitat available for gorillas in the area.

Pygmy hunters, meanwhile, say that in recent months they have encountered increasing numbers of dead gorillas and chimpanzees in the forest, where they have been felled by a mysterious affliction.

"You can hardly find any live gorillas anymore," said Mr. Mikou (Hilarion Mikou, a pygmy hunter). "We've never seen this before. A big game animal that fears nothing is just dropping dead."[10]

War

Deforestation brings gorillas into closer contact with the human population and forces them to share the impact of human problems. Civil war in several central African countries has brought added hardship and suffering to gorilla as well as human populations. In the 1990s renewal of an age-old conflict in Rwanda brought conservation efforts almost to a standstill throughout west central Africa. Conflict between the two major tribes of Rwanda, the Hutu and the Tutsi, is not new, but its escalation since 1990 has been catastrophic. From 1990 to 1993 Tutsi rebels calling themselves the Rwanda Patriotic Front invaded Rwanda from

Refugees of the Rwandan civil war are expelled from neighboring Zaire. The ongoing civil strife in many areas of Africa has halted conservation efforts.

bases they had established in neighboring Uganda. In 1994 war between the two tribes again broke out on a scale that left Rwanda shattered and neighboring countries burdened with fleeing refugees. At least a half-million Rwandans died and 3 million more fled the country to live in sub-poverty conditions in refugee camps in Tanzania, Zaire, and Uganda. As many as three thousand people a day died of disease and starvation.

In 1996 civil war erupted in Zaire (formerly the Belgian Congo) and more than a million refugees were again on the move. In 1997 Zaire established a new government under the name Democratic Republic of the Congo. Before the year was over the country was again engaged in conflict, and the fighting flared once again in the summer of 1998. The entire west-central region of Africa continues to suffer from hunger, disease, and political instability. With people problems this serious, concerns about wildlife and the environment take a backseat.

Death, devastation, and loss

Gorillas and other wildlife have suffered. Land mines, bands of soldiers, and piles of disease-bearing human medical waste, dumped by soldiers and refugees, fill many forests including some national parks. There is no money to maintain the national parks. Soldiers took over or destroyed many park buildings. The park headquarters in Rwanda's portion of the Virunga Volcanoes park is a roofless ruin. Rwanda's successful tourism program is no longer in operation. Park rangers left because they feared for their lives or because there was no money to pay them. International conservation organizations continue to operate, but often they cannot even enter the areas where gorillas are most threatened. In a July 1997 news release the World Wide Fund for Nature reported on Congo's section of the Parc National des Virunga, "In the last two years, 44 park guards have died while in service at Virunga as well as 12 of the highly endangered mountain gorillas."[11] Dian Fossey's Karisoke Research Center is a shambles with scientists attempting to continue their work from nearby communities.

Hundreds of thousands of refugees live in crude camps on the fringes of the forests set aside as state parks. Their needs are desperate and immediate. They need wood for cooking fires and shelters. Most take only what they need on a daily basis, but the need is neverending. Tree by tree they encroach on the parks.

Some of the refugees are turning to parkland for more than their personal needs. *Gorilla Conservation News* reported that

> a considerable number of Rwandan refugees in North-Kivu, eastern Zaire, has specialized in the trading of natural resources (coal, wood, wild game etc.) which they obtain entirely from the Virungas National Park. According to the report of Nicolas Blondel, representative of the European Union in Zaire, Rwandan refugees have cut approximately half of Mt. Mikeno's bamboos to manufacture and sell derived products such as mats, fans, baskets, etc.[12]

The report states that evidence of the activities' effect on the gorillas is hard to determine without long-term observations. It is noted, however, that some groups have changed their annual traveling pattern, spending only two months in the bamboo area rather than the usual three.

The overwhelming human problems plaguing central Africa draw attention and resources away from wildlife conservation. Saving the gorilla requires first solving some of the human problems and controlling the destruction of the forests. Steps are being taken to save the forest by regulating its use, but many conservationists fear that it is too little too late.

CITES

Some international groups attempt to regulate the forest destruction and the trade in endangered species by using already existing treaties, but success depends on the cooperation of all involved. Logging companies, governments, and the end consumer must all be willing to make sacrifices and abide by established guidelines.

One such treaty, known as CITES, the Convention on International Trade in Endangered Species of Wild Fauna and Flora, went into force on July 1, 1975. The signing

countries agreed that they would monitor trade in plants and animals among themselves. They listed and rated plants and animals according to their numbers and the stability of their species. For example, List 1 includes those species in which any trade at all is likely to affect their survival. The lists are published in a series of books called the *Red Data Books*. CITES now has a membership of 143 countries. It is the responsibility of each country to enact and enforce laws to restrict the importation of endangered species across its borders.

A bulldozer shovels corpses into a mass grave near Goma, Zaire. As human suffering continues in central Africa, vital resources necessary for protecting the gorilla are diverted to humanitarian efforts.

The Endangered Species Act

In the United States the conventions of CITES can be enforced under the Endangered Species Act of 1973. This act provides broad protection for species of fish, wildlife, and plants that are listed as threatened in the United States or elsewhere. It specifies criminal penalties of up to $50,000, imprisonment of one year, or both. The Endangered Species Act has helped to limit the importation of

Gorilla hands and a skull are displayed for sale at a market stall in Africa.

endangered apes into the United States, but importers continue to smuggle in both live animals and animal parts.

The International Primate Protection League reports that

> On June 25, 1998 William Stevens, owner of the Evolution store at 12 Spring Street, NY, was sentenced to 16 months in federal prison for wildlife smuggling with a concurrent 12 month sentence for trafficking in Native American remains. Stevens was charged with multiple violations of the CITES, the Endangered Species Act, the Migratory Bird Treaty Act, and the Native American Grave Protection and Repatriation Act. [Among the items seized were two gorilla skulls and two gorilla foot ashtrays.]

Commenting on the case Agent Ed Grace of the U.S. Fish and Wildlife Service said illegal wildlife trafficking is one of the major causes of worldwide wildlife loss. In monetary gain, the $2 billion to $3.5 billion a year industry exceeds illegal arms dealing and is surpassed only by drug smuggling.[13]

The Forest Stewardship Council

Another organization involved in protecting the forest environment is the Forest Stewardship Council (FSC). The FSC has introduced a labeling plan for forest products to give consumers a guarantee that the product comes from a well-managed forest. The FSC logo on a product certifies that it comes from a forest that meets the internationally recognized FSC Principles and Criteria of Forest Steward-ship. To meet the criteria logging companies must manage the forest in a sustainable manner. They must harvest forest products responsibly without destroying the entire forest, and trees must be replanted for the future.

Some companies, such as African Charcoal (AFCHAR), are striving to come into compliance with accepted envi-ronmental standards. AFCHAR produces charcoal only from timber resources that have been planted by man. AFCHAR's objective is to obtain FSC accreditation for all its manufac-turing plants. They have also hired a full-time environmen-tal officer with experience in forestry.

Right now, no timber coming out of Africa is FSC certi-fied. Certification will only become important to logging companies when governments refuse to allow noncertified forest products to be imported into their countries. CITES and FSC cannot enact or enforce international law. They can only develop guidelines, improve public education, and encourage responsible harvesting. Corruption, mismanage-ment, and disinterest within the member governments limit their effectiveness. Consumers can cause changes through both boycotts of noncertified products and expressions of public outrage over abuses. Governments burdened with huge debts are tempted to ignore violations or push for cer-tification even though the logging operation does not meet FSC standards. A vigilant and responsible public can sway their decision.

Debt-for-nature swaps

Many countries with rainforests also have huge amounts of debt. Their international creditors calculate that the likelihood of repayment is more or less remote. Some sell the debt to the highest bidder and write off the rest. Conservation organizations can buy these debts and free the country from the obligation to repay them. For example, if an African country owes a European bank a million dollars, a conservation group might agree to buy the debt by paying the bank half that amount. The African country still owes the money, but now they owe it to the conservation group. The conservation group can agree to forgive the debt in return for the establishment of a national park. The country must provide the money to run the park. This costs far less than repaying the original debt, and wildlife benefits as well.

A bamboo rainforest rises in the lush landscape of Rwanda's Parc des Volcans. Various organizations are working to preserve such areas for future generations.

Is it working?

All of these efforts are steps in the right direction, but the forest continues to fall at an alarming rate. Dr. Debra Forthman, editor of *African Primates,* says, "The few at-

"We've decided to destroy your habitat, but maybe I can get you a job around here."

tempts to control deforestation are, in my opinion, ineffective. Pressure must somehow be brought to bear on the logging companies, mostly French, Italian, Belgian, which are conducting activities in Africa that would be illegal in their home countries."[14]

In a recent book based on his twenty-three years of research in the Kibale rainforest of Uganda, a Duke University biologist, Thomas Struhsaker, agrees that current methods are ineffective. He calls for radical changes in the way rainforests are managed. Struhsaker argues that not only must larger tracts of land be put in preserves, but harvesting practices must be changed drastically. He says, "The destruction of these forests is indisputably one of the greatest ecological disasters in the history of *Homo sapiens*."[15] Struhsaker's study examines the impact of logging on wildlife as well as commercial timber species. He points out that studies of the forests must consider all of the flora and fauna because the relationships are so complex.

Struhsaker believes that the only hope for long-term conservation of the forests is population control, energy conservation to reduce wood use, and strong forest management policies by stable governments. He suggests that the United States dole out foreign aid based on a nation's commitment to achieving these goals. Many conservationists fear that these goals cannot be reached in time to save the great apes of Africa. Conservationist Craig Sholley expresses his greatest fear as, "I am afraid that some day we will look back and say, 'My God, how could we let this happen . . .' and it will be too late."[16]

3

From Subsistence Hunting to the Bushmeat Crisis

All four species of great ape are in desperate trouble. It is my firm belief that if action is not taken now, there will be no viable populations of great apes living in the wild within 50 years.

—Jane Goodall

GORILLAS HAVE ALWAYS BEEN hunted by humans. Big-game hunters, specimen collectors, and native hunters have all stalked the huge apes. However, in an age when animals such as whales, elephants, and egrets were killed for ivory, oil, feathers, skins, or other by-products, the gorilla had limited economic value to humans. In recent years, though, political and economic changes in Africa have conspired to turn wild-game hunting into a major commercial enterprise and a serious threat to gorillas and other wildlife.

Sport and specimen hunters

In the early 1900s wealthy sportsmen flocked to Africa to bag the plentiful game found there. They were seeking adventure and trophies. Gorillas had a reputation as savage opponents, and their heads were highly prized trophies. Big-game hunters were not the only ones stalking gorillas. Zoos and natural history museums were gaining in popularity

A game hunter poses with his many trophies. During the early 1900s, African safaris were popular among wealthy hunters hoping to bag big game.

around the world. Zoos sought live specimens and museums desired stuffed ones for their displays. Often entire families of gorillas were killed to capture a single infant for the zoo trade. All too often the captured infant soon died. Live animals were also purchased by medical laboratories. As researchers became more aware of the similarities between humans and the great apes they recognized the benefit to medical research of experimenting with primate subjects.

Today sport hunters, zoos, and medical laboratories pose little threat to gorillas. Killing or exporting gorillas is illegal. Safaris go into the jungle armed with cameras, sketchpads, and binoculars instead of rifles. Tourist groups creep through the underbrush seeking only the thrill of watching a gorilla family munching on greenery. Responsible zoos and medical labs have their own breeding programs and no longer purchase great apes captured in the wild. Yet more gorillas are being killed by hunters than ever before.

Traditional hunting

For thousands of years many African tribes hunted the vast forests of central Africa. Sometimes they killed gorillas, but in small numbers by spear, net, and trap. In the highlands where the mountain gorilla lives, primates were not favored as food. In these areas gorillas were sometimes accidental by-catch of traps set for bushbuck, duiker, and other game animals. Often the gorillas died in the snares or were killed by the returning poachers. Others survived with serious injuries. Sometimes gorilla heads and hands were taken to city markets for sale to tourists as souvenirs. Occasionally gorillas were trapped for sale to live-animal markets such as zoos.

Lowland gorillas have traditionally been hunted for their meat by many forest-dwelling tribes, but these people hunted only to feed themselves and their communities. Traditional hunting methods were too inefficient to have much impact on the population. Hunters searched for animal signs, then set snares or waited in the brush with

Before modern hunting methods took hold, large game such as gorillas had to be removed from the forest by hand.

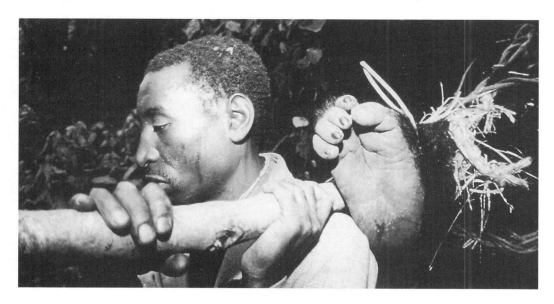

arrows or spears. It was a slow and dangerous process. Removing large game from the forest after it was killed was also slow and tedious. Operating in the dense forest was difficult and gorilla populations were not significantly affected. This way of life could have continued for many more years without having a serious impact on gorilla numbers, but change was coming to Africa.

Changing times

As more and more of the forest was cleared both wildlife and human forest dwellers were forced into smaller areas, or caused to flee deeper into the hinterlands. Several African countries became concerned about the effect on wildlife and set aside huge tracts of land as national parks.

The parks gave plant and animal species a place of refuge, but conservationists from both inside and outside Africa failed to see the tribal peoples as a natural part of the ecosystem. Their needs and lifestyles were not considered. The result was anger and misunderstanding on both

A snare is inspected by members of an antipoaching patrol at the Karisoke Research Center in Rwanda's Virunga Mountains.

sides. Native hunters continued hunting the land as they had always done, but many of their traditional hunting grounds were now parks under the protection of the state. Hunting in areas they had roamed for generations was now called poaching. The hunters felt that the forests belonged to them. They did not understand why they could not continue making their living as their fathers and grandfathers had done.

Even limited subsistence hunting took a toll on the mountain gorillas because their numbers were already low. By midcentury the mountain gorillas were seriously endangered and the loss of even a single animal was cause for concern. Gorilla researcher Dian Fossey took the plight of the mountain gorilla very personally. She and her crews destroyed hundreds of snares and aroused worldwide sympathy for the innocent victims of the poachers. But her emotional involvement made it impossible for her to see both sides of the issue. In the end she did little toward finding a real solution to the problem. Destroying snares has little lasting effect. There are always poachers waiting to set new ones.

Bushmeat

Fossey brought worldwide attention to the plight of the mountain gorilla, but 99 percent of all gorillas live in the vast lowland forests of west and central Africa. These gorillas were seldom seen by Western man. They lived deep in the almost impenetrable swampy jungles. Although their meat was considered a delicacy by many of the forest-dwelling tribes, traditional hunting methods were too inefficient to have much commercial value. At midcentury this population was still strong and thriving.

With the influx of guns, the danger to the hunter was reduced and forest dwellers began to take out more gorilla meat than they could eat. At first they sold the excess to villagers who lived on the edge of the forest. They traded meat for grain, other farm products, and manufactured goods like pots and utensils. When the timber companies cut roads into the forests, they brought in logging workers

Drying bushmeat hangs on the exterior of a butcher shop in a makeshift logging village.

and their families, who built makeshift villages near the logging operations. These families needed meat, and hunting began to grow as a commercial enterprise.

In the 1990s the term "bushmeat" has come into popular use. Bushmeat refers to the meat of any wild animal that is hunted and sold in quantity. In a 1997 report on the bushmeat trade, Angela Meder found that logging camps were relying on bushmeat, including great apes, for much of their diet. She reports on one logging camp in the Bee Forest, Gabon, where observers discovered that "the provisions for the workers included 35 chimpanzees and three gorillas within a period of 2 months."[17] There are dozens of similar camps scattered through the forest and all need meat.

Poachers now own or lease high-powered rifles. Kills can be made quickly and from a much greater distance. Much of the forest has been cut down or burned, and logging roads now reach deep into the remaining jungle. The roads make bringing the game out of the forest much easier and faster. The drivers of logging trucks earn extra money by transporting the game in their trucks so that it reaches market much more quickly.

Though killing or capturing gorillas for any reason is now illegal, these activities pose a more serious threat than ever before to the survival of gorilla populations. Modern technology, human need, and greed have turned subsistence hunting into a deadly industry. The additional problems brought by civil war in Rwanda and Zaire (now the DRC) set the stage for disaster.

The bushmeat trade: a grave threat to lowland gorillas

As a result of war, exploitation, and poverty, poaching has blossomed into a major threat to wildlife. Bushmeat of all kinds is in high demand. Poaching is now a well-organized commercial venture, intensified by several kinds of social change. Populations are shifting. Farmers and cattle herders are being forced out of their homelands and their traditional lifestyles by war and forest clearing. Many are employed by logging companies and have established villages near the timber concessions. They need meat and have the money to buy it. Hundreds of thousands of hungry war refugees now also live in camps near the boundaries of the forest. The need for food in these camps has created a thriving market for bushmeat.

A gorilla hand smokes atop a grill, a gruesome example of the bushmeat trade.

In addition poachers have found an even better-paying market for their products. Sophisticated diners in city homes and restaurants across Africa, and in some European countries, have developed a taste for bushmeat. A report from the World Wide Fund for Nature says bushmeat from west and central Africa shows up on menus from Cameroon to Congo and even Brussels and Paris. People delight in the novelty and strong flavors and are willing to pay a price much higher than the price of beef or pork. They dine on gorilla steak and elephant chops without regard to the damage being done to endangered species.

Conservationists have estimated that approximately 20 percent of all bushmeat consists of primates. Many people don't realize that the game being taken includes large numbers of great apes, says Dr. Anthony Rose, an expert on the bushmeat crisis. Their continued existence is seriously threatened by this illegal hunting and trade. The growth of the bushmeat trade since 1990 has been staggering. Rose estimates that at that time approximately six hundred lowland gorillas were killed and eaten each year. Since then the bushmeat trade has grown into major business. Today it is estimated that at least that number of gorillas are being killed each year in the northern part of the DRC alone. A report published in 1998 by the Bushmeat Project estimates that

> this year a ragged army of 1,500 bushmeat hunters supported by timber industry infrastructure will illegally shoot and butcher more than 2,000 gorillas and 4,000 chimpanzees in the forest region of west and central Africa. That is four times the number of (mountain) gorillas on Rwanda's Mt. Visoke and 10 times more chimpanzees than live near Tanzania's Gombe Stream. People eat more great apes each year than are now kept in zoos and laboratories in North America.[18]

Accurate statistics on the full impact of illegal hunting on gorilla populations are difficult to compile. Poachers do not advertise their illegal activity, and conservationists and reporters are not allowed into many critical areas. Kelly Stewart, editor of *Gorilla Conservation News,* writes:

> A critical message to emerge from this year's issue is the serious threat that hunting poses to gorillas in certain regions of west and central Africa. Illegal hunting has reached alarming proportions in some countries and could possibly wipe out gorillas and other animals from particular areas. We urgently need data on the impact of hunting on gorilla populations, as well as stricter controls against poaching and the bushmeat trade.[19]

Illegal hunting now poses a serious threat to African wildlife including the great apes. In *New Scientist,* an on-line magazine, Laura Spinney writes, "Although primate meat accounts for only a fraction of the trade, hunting is now considered to be a greater global threat to primates in general, and great apes in particular, than the destruction of their forest habitat."[20]

John Robinson of the Wildlife Conservation Society says, "Great apes are particularly vulnerable, because they just don't have the reproductive capacity to bounce back."[21] Female gorillas give birth only once every three to four years and many offspring do not survive infancy, so animals killed by hunters are not easily replaced.

Existing laws should protect gorillas and other endangered species from hunters, but little effort is made to enforce laws, and corruption among government employees is common. Karl Ammann, a Swiss businessman and wildlife photographer who has lived in Africa for many years, reports that the endangered status of gorillas drives the price of the meat up but offers them no real protection:

> At the Conkouati Wildlife Reserve, we filmed a lorry being loaded with bushmeat, right next to an IUCN [World Conservation Union] vehicle. When we interviewed one of the traders and asked why the cost of the meat doubled by the time it reached the coastal town of Pointe Noire, we were told that the government rangers manning the road blocks would need to be paid. When we asked how much, we were told the more protected the species the higher the price.[22]

Ammann also tells of a police chief in Cameroon with a taste for bushmeat. The chief sent a gun and cartridges to poachers by "bush taxi." The poacher returned the gun along with most of a gorilla carcass. He was allowed to keep a small part of the meat in payment for his services. According to Ammann, "The bushmeat trade and forest exploitation are the gravest conservation crises facing Africa since the ivory crisis."[23]

A side effect of the bushmeat trade is renewed sales of captive infant gorillas as pets and zoo animals. However, according to Rose, most of the infants die before they can be sold, or they wind up in the stew pot along with their parents. He says infant gorillas alive or dead are a byproduct of killing the parents and are of little interest to the hunters.

A realist's choice isn't easy

CNN's Gary Strieker writes that he faced a difficult choice when a man with a captive infant gorilla offered to

The emaciated corpse of an infant gorilla lies in a battered suitcase in an abandoned logging camp.

sell it to him. The creature was weak from hunger and traumatized by its captors. Hunters had killed its mother the week before. He knew that some people buy orphaned apes and donate them to the Wildlife Rescue Center at the Limbe Zoo in Cameroon. Strieker believes that the only realistic way to protect the apes is to protect the forest where they live. Knowing that we can't save everything, the reporter looked at a hungry, frightened infant gorilla and made a difficult choice:

> I'm now a realist, accepting that most of the wild animals in the forest along the roads we've traveled will probably disappear in the next decade—and accepting that, I could not buy that baby gorilla.
>
> To do so would have encouraged the hunter to go out and capture another—and this one was already too traumatized to survive much longer.
>
> I'm a realist, but I still wonder if I did the right thing.[24]

The choices are never easy and advocacy for one choice or another is intense. Gary Strieker was moved by the infant gorilla and wanted to help, but he believed that buying animals from poachers was not the best way to help the species.

Talks with the hunters

Rose says he has interviewed poachers who claim that they look forward to a day when they can afford to go out of business. They say they do not enjoy the killing and are concerned about the future of the wildlife. Some express the desire to turn to another type of work, but they have families to care for and there is much money to be made in the bushmeat business.

Rose believes that many of these poachers would sincerely like to give up hunting and turn to other types of employment. To support this belief, he describes a recent trip to a hunting camp in Cameroon. Rose wanted to better understand the men who make their living by hunting. Joseph Melloh, a hunter, had been identified as a person who might be converted to work for conservation. Joseph took Rose to his hunting camp deep in the woods where they spent a week talking to hunters. Joseph claimed to have stopped killing gorillas, but he introduced Rose to hunters who admitted to killing gorillas and other apes.

Rose interviewed Davide, a hunter who had killed twenty gorillas in three months. When asked if he liked shooting gorillas, Davide replied, "Of course not. It is dangerous and very hard work. But if I find them, I must use the gun that my patron has given me for its purpose."[25] Davide told Rose that he is saving money and hopes to give up the hunting life one day.

Joseph has begun growing crops and looking for other ways to support his family. Rose made a contract with Joseph. He agreed to give him $120, enough money to support his family until his crops were ready for harvest. In exchange Joseph agreed to protect gorillas and other apes instead of hunting them. He also agreed to keep a journal and provide periodic reports of his activities. Rose writes:

> After making our agreement I felt a strong sense of relief. For days I had been struggling with a difficult conundrum. To help the apes required trusting the ape killers. As a professional from North America I needed reasonable proof that Joseph would not use this money to rent a gun, buy cartridges, and return to the hunt. As a person in the rainforest I had the man's word, and I knew that his word was as good as gold.[26]

In due time Joseph sent his first report, described by Rose:

Now there is a man in the forest of eastern Cameroon who is . . . striving in the face of odds to get through this hunting season and this year without killing apes or any other living being. . . . His most intriguing achievement from my viewpoint is illustrated in these four journal entries:

1 June: "I have left Bordeaux to visit Davide in his camp."

2 June: "Davide and I have gone to the forest where he used to hunt and we have met two groups of gorillas which I have asked him not to shoot. He accepted not to kill them. I have spent the night there with him in the forest. . . ." [Davide killed some monkeys to sell for meat.]

3 June: "Davide and I have passed another night in the forest."

4 June: "I have left Davide's camp and I am with my family in Bordeaux."

If Joseph did convince Davide not to shoot gorillas in the forest, it is a promising sign. The two men could have made $60 to $80 by butchering and selling a silverback from each group. The $20 per week that I advanced Joseph does not match such an economic incentive. I believe that the two men

Tribesmen squat beside the body of an enormous ape in this 1920s-era photo. Today tribes must find other ways to meet their economic and survival needs if the gorilla is to survive.

envisioned something better in their future; some benefit that can come from saving gorillas rather than killing them. And we can say with reasonable confidence that two great apes were spared the bullet, at least for a while, because of our small intervention.[27]

The apparent success of this modest intervention supports Rose's belief that the best way to stop the slaughter is by forming partnerships with the people who are involved. He stresses the point that hunters, meat traders, truck drivers, logging executives, police, and consumers must all be given the opportunity to be part of the solution rather than part of the problem: "It is in partnership with these people that we will find alternative ways to satisfy the human needs that drive the destructive commercial trade in wildlife bushmeat. . . . This work cannot be done alone or in conflict. We must collaborate to save the great apes."[28]

The Ape Alliance

Conservation groups have recognized the value of collaboration among themselves as well as with local governments and communities. In early 1998, thirty-four conservation groups joined to form the Ape Alliance, a coalition to seek a solution to the effect of illegal hunting of ape populations. Ian Redmond, chairman of the alliance, says they are not trying to bring about changes in the law because the animals are already protected by the laws of the countries involved. However, the governments don't have the resources to control the illegal hunting and trade. According to Redmond the bushmeat trade is out of control and he calls for assistance from the logging companies. He asserts, "At the very least, the logging companies must ensure that their work force obeys the law."[29]

The alliance is calling for timber companies to police their own employees and seek certification of their products by an independent body such as the Forest Stewardship Council. The FSC logo on a product guarantees the purchaser that the timber comes from forests that are managed for the protection of both wildlife and indigenous peoples.

Some timber companies are already attempting to provide food for their workers so they don't have to depend on bushmeat as a protein source. Hinrich Stoll says his company, CIB, imports cattle to feed its workers and is considering building fish ponds. He argues, however, that they are timber people and cannot be expected to be experts in agroforestry. He claims that his requests for support from groups such as the World Conservation Union (IUCN) have been ignored: "It is a very complex matter, but it can only be solved in close collaboration with the population. A foreign company cannot play the role of police alone."[30]

Anthony Rose agrees that collaboration between all parties involved—the timber companies, local governments, native peoples, conservation organizations, and consumers worldwide—is essential. He believes that such cooperation is possible and it is not too late to save the gorillas in all the unprotected forests:

> It is vital that we strive to save them, and mourn the loss of each ape killed in this illegal business. But at the same time, we must help the people of the African forest, village and town to make a life that honors their traditional reverence for wildlife. These Africans did not invent the guns, roads, and chain saws that are destroying their natural heritage. We who bring these harsh tools to Africa are obliged to curb their destructive use. The future of ape and man depends on it.[31]

4

Gorilla Tourism: Gorillas Pay Their Own Way

With all the apes I've seen in the wild, there's nothing that compares to sitting in a glade and watching a family of mountain gorillas. They're beautiful creatures . . . so gentle.

—Michael Nichols, *The Great Apes*

THE CONFLICT BETWEEN human needs and the needs of wildlife is never easy to resolve. Governments and conservation organizations face heartrending questions with no easy answers. Across Africa whole populations have been displaced by war and famine. Children are starving. Families are homeless. Disease races unchecked through villages and refugee camps. By comparison the cause of the remaining gorillas seems less important.

Steuart Dewar, who with his wife Jane is involved in gorilla conservation and protection, puts it this way: "Conservation is a sophisticated concept. People can only become concerned about environmental issues when their own basic needs have been met. People who are struggling to provide food and shelter for their families cannot be expected to find the time or energy to care about gorillas."[32] For that reason, he says, money and incentive for conservation must come from more affluent countries.

Starving African children, some too weak to stand, congregate to receive food handouts.

A pilot tourism program

Conservationist Craig Sholley shares Dewar's view. Sholley is a conservationist who spent more than twenty years studying the mountain gorilla. He worked to convince local governments to stop clearing the rainforest to create more farmland. In a telephone interview Sholley stated, "So many real people problems exist in the area that it is hard to focus on wildlife. If there is any hope of saving the mountain gorilla, the money must come from outside sources."[33]

Even with outside money, conservation programs can succeed only through the goodwill and support of local governments and people. In the late 1970s, three conservation organizations—the African Wildlife Foundation, the World Wildlife Fund, and England's Fauna and Flora Preservation Society—began discussions with the Rwandan government. The goal was to find a way to give people an incentive to save the gorillas by making them more valuable alive than dead. The plan was to bring paying guests to see the gorillas. Through photos and media reports of Dian Fossey's work, the world felt a connection with the mountain gorillas, and wealthy tourists were willing to pay a lot of money to see the huge apes foraging in their native forest.

So the first gorilla tourism program was born in Rwanda as the Mountain Gorilla Project (MGP). The project consisted of a three-pronged plan dedicated to antipoaching, tourism, and education. The MGP was financed by the three conservation organizations, and Jean Pierre von de Becke was its first director.

It took several years to complete preparations for the first tourists. Gorilla groups were studied and identified, then an appropriate group was selected and habituated. The term *habituate* describes the process of accustomizing the gorillas to having humans nearby. Gorillas are gentle and peace-loving, but if they feel threatened they will protect their family. They had to gradually accept the idea that humans nearby did not present a danger to their family.

Guides and trackers made daily trips into the forest to follow the group of gorillas through its daily routine. They practiced behavior that the gorillas recognized as submissive and nonaggressive. Gradually they moved closer to the gorilla group. In time the gorillas were comfortable with several humans observing them from as little as fifteen feet away. The goal was to observe, without interfering with the gorillas or changing their behavior.

That was not always easy. Young gorillas, like young humans, are curious and mischievous. Much like human teenagers, they want to investigate anything that is new and different. Sometimes they come too close to the visitors. They may even attempt to touch clothing or camera gear.

Although these encounters can be exciting for both the humans and the gorillas, they are discouraged for several reasons. Gorillas are very susceptible to human illnesses. Individuals who show obvious signs of illness are not allowed to visit the gorillas, but diseases are sometimes contagious when there are no noticeable symptoms. Therefore, a minimum distance must be maintained between the humans and the apes. That distance was set at five meters (about fifteen feet) from the gorillas. There is also the chance that, by coming too close, a tourist might inadvertently violate gorilla etiquette and cause an aggressive confrontation. Finally, gorillas are wild animals. Interaction between gorillas and humans can change their natural behavior. Visitors are instructed to slowly back away if a gorilla approaches nearer than the five-meter limit. Occasionally guides have to resort to shaking a twig at a curious youngster if it insists on coming too close.

Other preparations

Habituation of the gorilla group was only one step taken to prepare for the tourists. The area was studied and mapped. Guides were hired and trained to track gorillas through the forest. They also learned to understand gorilla behavior and etiquette. Some of them had to learn English, the most common language of the tourists. Sometimes the behavior of foreign tourists could be more baffling than gorilla behavior. So the guides were taught how to interact with the tourists. They learned to prevent the tourists from accidentally doing anything that would seem threatening to the gorillas, while also assuring that each visitor had a rewarding and safe experience.

A curious young gorilla touches the hat of a researcher at the Karisoke Research Center in Rwanda.

In the meantime, conservationists Amy Vedder and Bill Weber were developing educational programs for both local residents and tourists. The local people were taught how the new program would work and how they could benefit from it. Tourists had to learn about the gorillas, and what to expect when they went into the forest to see them. Some of the guides were trained in presentations on gorilla life and etiquette in both their native language and English.

A local guide educates tourists about gorilla behavior and habitat. Ecotourism has proved to be an important source of income for countries such as Rwanda.

To complete the preparations for the project, a strong regulatory unit was developed. Rangers and antipoaching patrols were organized to protect the valuable resources of the park and control poaching and other exploitative behavior. Finally, in the early 1980s the preparations were complete. The gorillas had been habituated, and six tourists a day could visit the group. As the success of the project became apparent, other gorilla groups were habituated. In all, four groups were eventually habituated, so a total of twenty-four tourists a day could observe gorillas.

Reaping the benefits

The twenty-four available tourist slots were usually filled well in advance. With the visitors came foreign money and a much-needed boost to the local economy. Many natives had jobs at salaries higher than the amount they could make farming or raising cattle. They worked as guides, trackers, park rangers, and members of antipoaching patrols. Others sold goods and services to the foreign visitors.

The years of preparation quickly paid off. By the late 1980s, gorilla tourism was Rwanda's third highest source of income, behind tea and coffee. The gorillas also benefited. Their numbers began a steady increase. In a three-year period the number of mountain gorillas in the Virunga range increased from around 285 to more than 300. According to Craig Sholley, who became director of the MGP in 1987, tourism had a dramatic impact on habitat preservation: "Not one inch of rainforest in the park was lost during the 1980s, the peak years of tourism in Rwanda."[34]

At first, the local community expressed doubts about the benefits of tourism. Soon after tourist visits were begun, local residents were surveyed. Only 30 percent agreed that the effort was a good thing for the park and believed that they would benefit from it. Five years later when the survey was repeated, 80 percent responded favorably to the same questions.

Besides the economic benefits, tourism produced an unexpected bonus—gorilla pride. People who had seen the animals only as competition for available land were now proud of their gorillas. The country blossomed with posters, signs, and even postage stamps promoting the apes. Gorillas became part of the national identity of Rwanda.

War in Rwanda

In the early 1990s the flourishing program was successfully turned over to the Rwandan National Park Service for administration. Six months later war broke out. On the effects of the war, Sholley says, "It has been devastating. Some gorilla groups are still being visited in Rwanda, but with no consistency. It is not safe. For all practical purposes the Rwanda program, which was the model for all others, has been shut down with little hope of things changing in the near future."[35]

Due to the tourism program the people of Rwanda have feelings of pride and ownership of the gorillas, and have made an effort to protect them from the fighting. But without the financial support brought by the tourist dollars the park is understaffed and in bad condition. The war has greatly increased the levels of human need and suffering. Poaching has increased because of the hundreds of thousands of hungry refugees in Rwanda and neighboring countries. The refugees have also contributed to habitat destruction because of their need for wood for building and firewood. Once again human needs have forced the needs of wildlife to take a backseat.

Even when the war and political crisis are over, rebuilding tourism will be a long slow process. Park buildings have been destroyed. There is still danger of land mines in the forest, though the Rwandan government and its people

Two charred corpses attest to the devastation of the Rwandan civil war. The raging war has forced the shutdown of Rwanda's gorilla tourism program.

have displayed great courage trying to rid the park of the mines. The mines present grave danger of injury to gorillas, tourists, and park employees. It will also take some time to prepare the gorillas for tourists again. Some of the habituated groups have broken up. War in other central African countries has caused the death of a number of gorillas, including several habituated silverbacks. However, in Rwanda both private citizens and the government have tried hard to protect their gorillas from the ravages of war. Only one Rwandan silverback has died and that death was accidental. Nonetheless, the habituation process will have to begin again. Some rangers and guides remain in the area hoping to return to work, but many new ones will have to be recruited, outfitted, and trained.

Other countries follow suit

Although Rwanda's tourism program may be foundering due to war, ecotourism is still the most successful method of reconciling conservation and human needs. Ecotourism and gorilla tourism programs modeled after Rwanda's pilot program continue to spread across Africa. Due to cooler temperatures and less-densely forested mountain slopes the mountain gorillas are more accessible than their lowland brothers. Like Rwanda, Uganda and the DRC are home to mountain gorillas. Both countries soon followed Rwanda's lead and developed their own gorilla-viewing programs.

In the DRC three gorilla groups were recently habituated near the Odzala National Park. However, the DRC is one of the most expensive countries in Africa, and Odzala is two days of difficult travel from the capital. So the cost to tourists in dollars, time, and hardship is significantly increased. In addition, local political unrest and security concerns have hampered the effort. There is little hope of real success unless the country becomes more politically stable.

Ecotourism: a broader view

Uganda, on the other hand, is developing a thriving ecotourism business. Ecotourism can be defined as environ-

Signs welcome visitors to the mountain gorilla preserve at Tshivanga Station in the DRC's Kahuzi-Biega National Park.

mentally responsible travel to natural areas for the purpose of appreciating nature. True ecotourism must follow some basic guidelines. Wildlife and their habitats must not be disturbed. Any impact that tourism has on the area must be within sustainable limits. In other words, it must not cause more damage than the environment can easily absorb. Waste disposal must be managed responsibly. The lifestyles and customs of other cultures must be respected, and conservation goals and education should be promoted. Responsible ecotourism allows people to enjoy natural areas while preserving them for future generations.

Uganda incorporates gorilla visits into its comprehensive ecotourism programs. Currently there are two groups of gorillas that tourists can visit. Only one can be booked in advance. Visitors to this group are limited to six tourists per day for a one-hour visit. Craig Sholley plans and sometimes directs tours to Uganda for an international tourism company. He says the gorillas are a big attraction, but the tours offer much more than gorilla viewing. These excursions take in much of the natural diversity of Uganda's environment. Visitors see many primates and other large mammals plus countless species of birds. They visit savannah, bush, and lake ecosystems in addition to the forested homes of mountain gorillas.

Viewing lowland gorillas

Until recent years, gorilla viewing was limited to the mountain ecosystems of Rwanda, Uganda, and the DRC. The lowland gorilla lives in the dense steamy jungles of low-lying rainforests. These areas are not ideal for wildlife viewing. The mountain technique of tracking the animals through the forest cannot be used in the swamps and thick tropical foliage. Recently the west African country of Gabon has recognized opportunity in its population of lowland gorillas and other large mammals. Gabon tourism officials use studies of feeding ecology to provide a way to work around some of the restrictions of the swampy jungle habitat of the lowland gorilla. Researchers and tour developers study feeding habits and learn the locations and seasons of favorite food sources. Footpaths and observation

Rwandan guides in a mountain gorilla sanctuary proudly pose for a photograph. Such guides have extensive knowledge of local plant and animal species.

posts are then built to the area of a "magnet" tree or grove. Few tourists actually see gorillas at these sites, but they are likely to see night nests, feeding signs, and tracks. Gabon is making excellent use of this approach in the Lope Reserve. Although the possibility of seeing gorillas is a major draw for tourists, the Lope is marketed as ecotourism rather than gorilla tourism. Gorilla sightings cannot be guaranteed, but the guides' knowledge of plants and animals and local history make the tours truly educational. Kelly Stewart, editor of *Gorilla Conservation News,* writes:

> Across Africa, ecotourism and gorilla-viewing tourism continue to be the most effective method of "sustainable use" being developed by conservation programs. In Gabon, . . . the success of ecotourism played a role in the official creation of a totally protected core area within Lope Reserve. Despite the advantages of tourism for conservation, we are all aware of its drawbacks and the need for constant monitoring of its effects.[36]

What are the drawbacks?

Conservationists agree that even the most effective tourism programs have their problems. Always uppermost in the minds of conservationists is the fear of introducing disease into the population. An epidemic in an already endangered species could be catastrophic. The chimpanzees of the Gombe Stream Reserve are an unfortunate example of the effects of exposure to human illnesses. The chimpanzees have contracted polio and have suffered fatal epidemics of other human diseases.

In an article in *African Primates,* Thomas M. Butynski and Jan Kalina cite an article published in the April 1994 issue of *Getaway* magazine to prove that tourism rules are sometimes flaunted by tour guides:

> The author of the article describes a close (1 m) encounter with a gorilla in the Bwindi Impenetrable Forest. The photographs in the article show a tourist in Zaire surrounded by gorillas that are within arm's reach. Physical contact was later made. The photographs suggest that the photographer was also within 1–2 m of the gorillas. According to the many tourists to the Zaire gorillas whom we have interviewed over the years, this is not an unusual encounter.

Close human-gorilla contact is a long-standing concern. We encourage those governments and conservation organizations who are managing, supporting and advising on gorilla tourism, to do more to ensure that the "5 m [15 feet] distance regulation" is strictly enforced.[37]

Although close encounters between humans and gorillas can be incredibly exciting for humans, they can cause irreparable harm to the wild species.

Another drawback is the concern that, in spite of precautions, the presence of the tourists may change the way gorillas behave. Anthropologist Kelly Stewart advocates balancing groups habituated for tourism with other groups that are visited only by researchers. Comparing the two groups will tell researchers if tourism is changing the gorillas. This is the approach taken in Rwanda and is unique in Africa. However, it can be argued that the presence of scientists may also affect the natural behavior of the apes.

Regulation and monitoring are the keys to success, but there are always people more interested in dollars than gorillas. They ignore the regulations and push to increase the number of visits allowed to the gorillas. Authorities working to establish gorilla-tourism programs that benefit both humans and gorillas must constantly resist pressure groups interested only in profit.

There is also some concern that the tourism business has produced changes in the daily duties and priorities of the park rangers. Much of their time is devoted to managing the problems caused by the large number of visitors to the parks. Sometimes the rangers don't have enough time to control poaching and illegal woodcutting. An article in the December 1997 issue of *Gorilla Journal* supports this argument:

> In July 1997 the number of visitors to the habituated gorillas in Uganda was exceptionally high, since gorilla tourism in Rwanda and the Democratic Republic of Congo was temporarily halted at that time.
>
> This has led to tremendous pressure on Mgahinga and Bwindi [two national parks where gorillas are visited by tourists]. At times there have been up to 5 overland lorries waiting on standby lists for gorilla permits in Mgahinga and Bwindi. The wardens of both parks are trying to deal with pressure from pushy tourists and tour guides/drivers who attempt bribery to convince park staff to allow double visits and extra visitors above the limit. . . . It puts the gorillas at risk. IGCP [International Gorilla Conservation Program] is working on a programme of education for tourists, especially the overland lorry companies, in an attempt to reduce the incidence of corruption.[38]

Sustainable Use

The theory of conservation through sustainable use is very controversial. Sustainable use means using something without using it up. There are two types of sustainable use programs: consumptive and nonconsumptive. Consumptive use means allowing a certain number of animals to be removed from a managed environment. They can be harvested for food, or for products such as leather or ivory, or they can be captured and sold as zoo animals, pets, or laboratory animals. Those in favor of this approach believe that limited legal harvesting gives economic value to the animals, which gives people an incentive to manage the animals wisely as a resource.

Others do not believe wildlife can be profitably managed. They fear that any relaxation of laws regulating the use of the animals will open the door to widespread poaching and corruption. Animal rights groups see it as a moral issue and feel strongly that this type of use of any animal is wrong.

Nonconsumptive sustainable use programs are less controversial because they do not involve killing or removing animals from the wild. These programs seek ways to give economic value to the animals without removing them from their ecosystem. Gorilla tourism and other ecotourism programs are examples of nonconsumptive sustainable use. The animals benefit the local economy while still living in the wild. However, according to some scientists any intrusion into their environment endangers the animals.

Some people feel that the animals are still exploited. Others believe that a balance can be maintained between conservation and human interests. They see this as the only realistic way to protect a species.

Most villagers in the areas affected by tourism recognize and enjoy the increased job opportunities and other economic benefits the tourist trade has brought. However, support is not universal. Some natives resent the intrusion of foreigners and believe that they have received no benefit from the program. They resent any restrictions on their traditional use of the forests.

The war has made still another problem apparent. Habituated gorillas do not fear humans. This trust in humans can put them in grave danger. In Rwanda both sides have made a sincere effort to protect the gorillas from the fighting, but people in other countries are not as protective. Soldiers and poachers armed with rifles have killed a number of habituated gorillas. An African Wildlife Foundation report describes the death of one silverback:

> When Rugabo, the dominant silverback male of a group of gorillas, was killed in August 1995, the world lost one of its most tourist-friendly gorillas. Rugabo had allowed tourists to visit his group for over 10 years. . . . He was a very gentle gorilla who touched the hearts of many people.
>
> Rugabo was killed with an AK-47 rifle. He was shot through the heart along with a female from his group. It appears from investigations that they were killed in order to capture a young gorilla. The killers were not able to sell the infant once they had caught him. He was released into a field and later to be found by park guards. The young gorilla recognized the guards because they had been patrolling Rugabo's group for years. He ran up to them and they were able to return him to his group.[39]

A park ranger talks with tourists in Rwanda's Parc des Volcans. Some conservationists worry that ecotourism will force park rangers to spend less time protecting gorillas and more time supervising tourists.

In spite of these drawbacks, most villagers, conservationists, and government officials agree that tourism is the best option at this time. It brings money into the local economy, thereby giving value to the gorillas and their habitat. It also builds a feeling of pride and ownership in the local population as the gorillas and the rainforest become a part of their national identity.

The tourists, who come from all over the world, take home with them a more enlightened view of Africa and its treasures. Theo Michael Schmitt wrote of his experience with the gorillas:

> My visit to the gorillas was unbelievably splendid and inspiring. . . .When the guide called for us to return after we had spent exactly one hour with the gorillas, we departed in a very melancholic mood. We walked back through the slippery undergrowth to the camp, first silently, then whispering. After the emotion and tension had relaxed somewhat, we exchanged our lively impressions. A young stock broker from New York even said, with tears in his eyes, "this was like a climb into paradise." [40]

5

Humans and Gorillas: Facing an Uncertain Future

Human kind projects onto animals its desires and fears and in the end observes mainly the fiction it has created. In the black countenance and tremendous strength of the gorilla it sees less an animal than a myth, a mysterious and monstrous image of itself.

—George Schaller, *Gorilla*

THE FIRST SCIENTIFIC STUDY of gorillas, conducted in 1959 by George Schaller, brought to light the fact that the species was already in serious trouble. The gorillas were then, and are today, being put at risk by human activity. An ever-growing human population is hungrily consuming the resources of central Africa, leaving the future of the gorilla and many other species of wildlife in serious doubt. Paradoxically, humans are also the gorilla's only hope for survival. Over the past forty years conservationists have committed countless dollars and man-hours to the fight to save the gorilla. Yet today, the mountain gorilla still teeters precariously on the brink of extinction, and the lowland varieties are facing the most serious threat ever to their continued existence.

Dr. Debra Forthman, director of Zoo Atlanta's field conservation program, says, "The prognosis for the mountain gorilla is, at best, guarded."[41] The already low numbers are further complicated by the fact that at present it is almost impossible for researchers and conservationists to enter the areas where the gorillas live. Karisoke Research Center was destroyed during the Rwandan civil war. Karisoke staff have moved their base of operations to a nearby community, but are rarely allowed into the forest to monitor the gorilla populations. Director Liz Williamson wrote from Karisoke in 1997:

> It was not in the best of circumstances that we marked, in 1997, the 30th anniversary of the establishment of the Karisoke Research Center (KRC). At present we are unable to enter the Volcanoes National Park. . . . Several of our most skilled trackers, including Nemeye Alphonse, were arrested in April and are still in prison waiting for their cases to come to trial. Tragically, we have lost long-term employee Nshogoza Fidele, who was killed by . . . [rebel soldiers] at his home on August 12, 1997. Our remaining trackers face severe economic hardship as food prices have tripled. Many staff members have been robbed of all their personal belongings, and some have abandoned their fields as well as their homes.[42]

The data that the Karisoke staff has been able to collect under these adverse conditions indicate that increased poaching is seriously affecting the remaining mountain gorilla population.

 ## Gorilla Humor

Jane Dewar of Gorilla Haven once had the pleasure of visiting and communicating with the gorilla Koko, who communicates in sign language. At the time, the scientists at Gorilla Foundation were unsuccessfully attempting to breed Koko with Michael, her close companion. Jane said, "I immediately saw what the problem was. Even though Koko and Michael are not siblings, they were raised together and had a brother-sister kind of relationship. Of course, they wouldn't breed with each other. I proved my point when I talked to Koko. I said, 'Michael is a fine gorilla.' Koko responded in sign language, 'He is a toilet.' Now, if that is not a brother-sister kind of relationship, I don't know what is!"

Conservationists hold more hope for the lowland varieties, but only if habitat loss and illegal hunting can be brought under control. Otherwise they fear that the wild population could disappear in fifty years or less. Most conservationists agree that any remaining hope for the gorillas lies in working with the people and governments of Africa to solve some of the overwhelming problems facing the human population. People facing the ravages of famine, war, homelessness, and disease cannot be expected to take a serious interest in conservation issues until their own most basic needs have been met.

Tutsi refugees find sanctuary within the confines of a Catholic seminary. The horrific social conditions in Rwanda have placed enormous burdens on the government, overshadowing conservation efforts.

Should the gorillas be saved?

Some people question the wisdom of devoting so much energy and money to the fight to save the gorilla, especially in light of the needs of the human population. They argue that throughout the course of life on earth, species have evolved, reached their peak, declined, become extinct, and been replaced by other species. When a species can no longer adapt to a changing environment it disappears as a natural part of the evolutionary process. Some people believe it should be allowed to happen unimpeded. However, until the twentieth century, it was a process that happened slowly over thousands or even millions of years. In the twentieth century humankind's conquest of technology has caused this process to escalate out of control.

Conservationists believe that humans, as the dominant species on earth, have a responsibility to the species that have been put at risk by human activities. They believe that to protect the future of all life on earth, humans must wisely manage their consumption of the earth's resources. The same forces that affect the gorillas of Africa or the tigers of India will eventually affect the human population. Rainforest destruction is already causing changes in the earth's weather patterns that cause drought in some areas and floods in others. So by preserving forests and wildlife, humans are protecting their own future.

A flagship animal

Charles Horton, curator of primates for Zoo Atlanta, says, "The gorilla is what we call a flagship animal. Their importance extends far beyond their own species."[43] He explains that most of the plants and animals in the gorilla's ecosystem are affected by the same forces that are putting the gorilla at risk. It is hard to get people interested in the fate of an insect, an invertebrate, or a forest fern. Yet these plants and animals play an important role in the delicate balance of life in the rainforest.

People respond to gorillas. Researchers get to know them individually by name, and the media introduces them to the world as individuals. We see ourselves reflected in their faces and their antics. People feel connected to gorillas and will fight to save them. Efforts to save the gorilla benefit the entire ecosystem. Therefore, the term *flagship animal* means the animal who carries the banner for all the rest. Even if the gorilla is lost, the fight will not have been in vain, because other wildlife will reap the benefits.

What is being done?

Dozens of organizations are working to protect the gorilla. Some, such as the World Wildlife Fund, are involved in global conservation efforts with departments devoted to gorillas and other great apes. Others focus their entire program on gorilla conservation; a few, such as the Dian Fossey Gorilla Fund, concentrate their efforts on the mountain gorilla subspecies.

This oversized birthday card for a young gorilla is just one example of how humans tend to individualize gorillas.

Conservation organizations accomplish much in direct conservation and education. They fight to have land set aside as parks or preserves, and they provide funds to support them. They monitor populations to determine which species are most endangered. Their educational programs bring worldwide awareness of conservation issues and the need for change. Through international campaigns they raise large amounts of money to support conservation.

There is a trend toward collaboration and pooling of resources among conservation groups. The recently formed Ape Alliance, involving thirty-four conservation groups in the fight against the illegal killing of great apes for the bushmeat trade, is one example. Three conservation organizations—the African Wildlife Foundation, the World Wildlife Fund, and England's Fauna and Flora Preservation Society—joined forces to start the Mountain Gorilla Project in Rwanda. In 1997 these same three organizations, and the wildlife authorities of the three countries that are home to mountain gorillas, began a cooperative effort called the International Gorilla Conservation Program (IGCP). The goal of the IGCP is to establish effective conservation and management of the forest shared by the three countries and to improve protection of mountain gorillas as a flagship species for this habitat.

Collaborations such as these help the various organizations to get more for their money and to stay abreast of what other groups are doing. Much of the conservation effort is directed toward habitat preservation and the control of illegal hunting. However, gorilla conservation efforts also include more direct intervention such as orphanages and veterinary clinics.

Gorilla orphanages

Orphaned animals are a by-product of the bushmeat trade. Gorilla orphans seldom survive, but several orphanages do what they can to increase their chances. These orphanages are almost always fully occupied. They no longer take an active role in trying to get illegally held animals confiscated, because they have no room for them. The Wildlife

Gorilla Haven

Deep in the North Georgia mountains a Chicago couple is doing their bit for captive gorillas. Jane and Steuart Dewar donated to causes supporting African conservation projects, but they wanted to do more. Jane Dewar says, "I just seem to have a natural rapport with gorillas. I understand them." The Dewars visited zoos around the world. They saw many gorillas in modern zoo habitats that appeared happy and well adjusted. Others seemed to be suffering from stress.

Many of these gorillas have spent most of their lives in small cages with no contact with other gorillas. Sometimes they were mistreated. Modern zoos allow their gorillas to live in family groups in naturalistic habitats. But some gorillas have been deprived of social contact with other gorillas for so long that they cannot adjust easily to the new lifestyle. Some developed unacceptable behavior patterns while they were confined to a cage.

The Dewars sold their Chicago home and business and bought 275 acres in the North Georgia mountains. The property included a cabin that was over one hundred years old. They renovated the cabin and moved into it. The Dewars plan to offer a place of refuge for captive gorillas. It will be a quiet place where overstressed gorillas can come to recover. The Dewars have hired a primatologist, well versed in the needs of gorillas, to run the facility. They hope to complete their preparations and welcome their first gorilla guest by the year 2000.

Rescue Center at Limbe and the Brazzaville Zoo, both in Congo, are two orphanages that care for orphaned gorillas. In June 1997 the Brazzaville facility had to be evacuated when fighting broke out in the city. A team of wildlife experts was allowed twenty minutes to tranquilize four gorillas with drug-tipped darts and load them into cages and vans. Man, a fourteen-year-old gorilla, had to be left behind because they had no cage large enough to transport him.

Not everyone believes that the orphanages benefit the species. Karl Ammann, an expert on the bushmeat crisis, says:

Increasing numbers of gorillas are orphaned as a result of the bushmeat trade. Gorilla orphanages have been established to care for these vulnerable animals; however, such centers are highly controversial.

Orphanages only deal with a by-product of the bushmeat trade, and many primatologists and conservationists even argue that they are a waste of money. The orphaned animals are classified as no longer being part of the wild gene pool, and so are biologically defunct.

It is also argued that the funding needed to look after a chimp [or gorilla] for 50 years could save far more animals by saving their habitat.[44]

Ammann, however, believes that orphanages can play an important role in the conservation effort as education facilities. He thinks they should be set up near urban centers where school classes can visit and interact with the apes.

Mountain Gorilla Veterinary Center

Since 1986 the Mountain Gorilla Veterinary Center (MGVC) has operated in Rwanda to monitor the health of wild gorillas and administer emergency medical care when necessary. The MGVC also cooperates with veterinarians and conservation workers from Uganda and Zaire in dealing with medical emergencies, such as snare removals. In addition to handling medical emergencies, the MGVC is conducting a study of gorilla health and, to this end, has collected fecal and urine samples from habituated gorillas.

Zoos

Historically, the primary image of zoos was not that of direct sponsors of conservation efforts, but modern zoos play an important role in wildlife conservation. Early zoos were for the amusement of people sheltered from the realities of the natural world. Zookeepers showed little concern for the needs of the animals. Most zoo animals were kept in small cages with concrete or wood floors. They were fed a diet very different from what they ate in the wild, and no thought was given to their social needs. Many gorillas spent their lives in tiny cages and never saw another gorilla.

Some zoos still operate this way, but they are the exception. Modern zoos and animal parks are open, beautiful places. The animals have abundant living space and interact with others of their species. Their environment mimics

As this 1944 photo reveals, early zoos were primarily amusement parks rather than wildlife conservation centers.

their natural habitat as closely as possible. Today progressive zoos give gorillas indoor and outdoor space and allow them to live in family groups. Of course, zoos can take this approach only so far. Space is always a factor, and the needs of the viewing public must be considered, as well. If people can't see the animals, they won't pay to come to the zoo, and the zoo can't stay in business.

Modern zoos are educational facilities with libraries, lecture rooms, and outreach programs. They provide an ideal forum for increasing public awareness of the need for conservation. Zoos also develop new veterinary techniques that can be adapted for use in the field, and knowledge gained from observing and studying breeding behavior of captive animals is used to increase the breeding potential of wild animals.

Modern zoos serve as important veterinary research facilities, enhancing science's understanding of gorilla physiology and behavior.

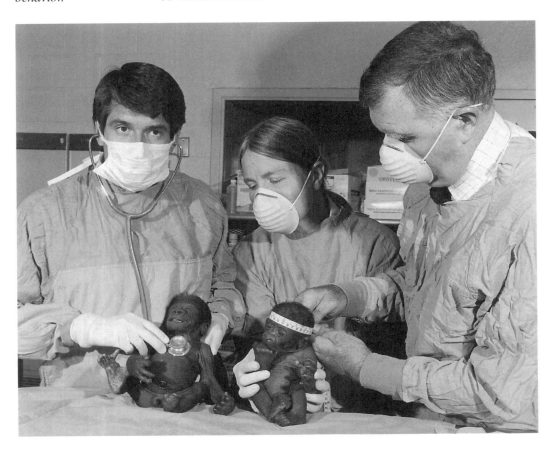

According to Robert M. McClung in his book *Last of the Wild,* gorillas have been successfully bred in captivity only since 1956, when the first recorded birth of a gorilla in captivity occurred at the Columbus Zoological Gardens in Ohio. Today over half the gorillas in zoos were bred in captivity. In 1995 the first test-tube baby gorilla was born at the Cincinnati Zoo. In vitro (test-tube) fertilization techniques may eventually be used to increase genetic diversity in small isolated populations.

According to the Captive Breeding Specialist Group (CBSG) of IUCN/SSC zoos and aquaria worldwide have an estimated 600 million visitors a year. The CBSG points out that this is potentially one of the largest conservation networks on earth. It stresses that to use the potential of this network, conservation must be a central theme of all progressive zoos and aquaria. Cooperation and partnerships between zoos and other conservation organizations worldwide are vital to the conservation of nature.

Conservation and research

Many zoos have their own conservation and field research programs and some, such as Zoo Atlanta and the Columbus, Ohio, zoo, publish journals on the status of both free-living and captive wildlife. Zoos are working closely with conservation organizations as well. Partners in Conservation (PIC), an organization that works to save the gorilla and its habitat, was established in 1991 by the staff and docents of Columbus Zoo. PIC not only works on projects that focus directly on gorillas, but develops and contributes to projects that improve the lives of the local people and involve them in conservation efforts. In collaboration with the Dian Fossey Gorilla Fund, they have contributed funds to the Karisoke Research Center to support antipoaching patrols and repair buildings damaged in Rwanda's civil war. They fund the yearly operating expenses of the Imbabazi Orphanage, which cares for 75 human children orphaned by the civil war. PIC also contributes to the Mountain Gorilla Veterinary Project by helping to fund the on-site training of Rwandan veterinarian Dr. Tony Muda-kikwa and contributing to the purchase of medical supplies.

PIC has formed an innovative partnership with local ar-tisans who produce handmade products such as masks and dolls for sale in the United States. The profits go back to Rwanda to help fund PIC's conservation projects there.

In Africa and around the world conservation groups are joining forces to fight for the protection of the gorilla, but not everyone agrees with their approach. Critics claim that most conservation organizations cave in too easily to local political pressure. They say they concentrate their efforts on setting up reserves and national parks, and avoid the big issues with political overtones such as the bushmeat trade. The critics agree that conservation groups do make suc-cessful contributions but they feel that the successes don't justify the amount of money spent to achieve them.

Conservationists, on the other hand, argue that they must walk a fine line. A harsh stand against local bureaucratic activity can cause them to be expelled from the country in question. A strong presence in the area and an active edu-cation program keep the eyes of the world focused on the issues and help prevent even more abuse. Therefore, they say, taking a too-firm stand with local governments would be self-defeating.

What does the future hold?

The steps being taken in the fight to save the gorilla are many-faceted. They range from educating a worldwide public to hand-feeding an infant gorilla in an orphanage. Conservation groups fight to halt habitat destruction and increase the size of protected areas. Solutions are being sought for political and economic problems that affect both humans and wildlife.

Africa's people problems are complex and cannot be re-solved quickly. Conservationist Karl Ammann believes the bushmeat crisis calls for immediate action. He proposes some short-term measures such as improved enforcement of existing laws; the killing of gorillas is against local law everywhere it is practiced, but enforcement is lax. He also

Anthropomorphism

Anthropomorphism is the practice of attributing human emotions and characteristics to animals. The scientific view is that animal behavior is based strictly on instinct and conditioning.

Primatologists, especially those studying the great apes, are often accused of anthropomorphism. Of her work with chimpanzees Jane Goodall said, "When, in the early 1960s, I brazenly used such words as 'childhood,' 'adolescence,' 'motivation,' 'excitement,' and 'mood,' I was much criticized. Even worse was my crime of suggesting that chimpanzees had 'personalities.' I was ascribing human characteristics to nonhuman animals and was thus guilty of that worst of ethological sins—anthropomorphism."

Primatologists studying the great apes usually distinguish one individual from another by giving them names—Digit, Rugabo, Flo, etc. This is also considered gross anthropomorphism. The scientific preference is to identify individuals with labels such as "juvenile male B16."

Although primatologists are still accused of anthropomorphism, their work is making it much harder for the scientific world to cling to the old belief that animals do not possess emotions. It is very difficult to explain the apparent emotions and relationships exhibited by the great apes in any other terms. Researchers argue, for example, that when the gorilla Koko described herself as feeling sad over the death of a pet kitten, there is no basis for assuming that she does *not* feel something very much like the sadness a human feels over losing a beloved pet. Currently there are no valid criteria for measuring the presence or absence of emotion in animals. Observation is the most reliable tool available, and observation often indicates the presence of feelings.

A caretaker playfully interacts with an infant gorilla. Primatologists and others who work with gorillas often attribute human characteristics to these nonhuman animals.

Activists from the environmental group Earth First! demonstrate on the steps of the Lincoln Memorial. By increasing public awareness, conservationists hope to improve the gorilla's plight.

advocates tightening of licensing procedures for guns, cartridges, and meat trading. Some success has already been achieved in removing from the market the cartridge used primarily to kill gorillas.

If the bushmeat trade is to be brought under control some alternative source of protein must be provided for people who rely on wild meat. Projects are being studied to breed and raise wild animals for sale as meat. Animals under consideration for breeding programs are species that are plentiful, hardy, and reproduce quickly such as the cane-rat. A cane-rat breeding facility is already in operation in Gabon.

Conservationists believe that hope for the gorilla lies in improved education and global awareness. It will require partnerships of diverse entities to find solutions to the related human problems. There is fear among conservationists that, if sweeping changes are not made in the near future, humankind's nearest kin, the great apes of Africa, the gorilla, the chimpanzee, and the bonobos may be fallen soldiers in the struggle to find ways for a small planet to provide for each member of a large and varied population.

Notes

Introduction

1. Quoted in Robert M. McClung, *Last of the Wild: Vanished and Vanishing Giants of the Animal World.* North Haven, CT: Linnet Books, 1997, p. 88.
2. George B. Schaller, "Gentle Gorillas, Turbulent Times," *National Geographic,* October 1995, p. 66.

Chapter 1: The Gorilla: The Largest Primate

3. Schaller, "Gentle Gorillas," p. 66.
4. Quoted in McClung, *Last of the Wild,* p. 88.
5. Jeffrey M. Masson and Susan McCarthy, *When Elephants Weep.* New York: Delacorte, 1995, p. 104.

Chapter 2: Deforestation and War

6. Schaller, "Gentle Gorillas," p. 67.
7. Laura Spinney, "Monkey Business," *New Scientist,* May 2, 1998, http://www.newscientist.com.
8. Quoted in Spinney, "Monkey Business."
9. Howard W. French, "An African Forest Harbors Vast Wealth and Peril," *Worldwide Forest/Biodiversity Campaign News,* from *New York Times,* April 3, 1996, http://forests.lic.wisc.edu/gopher/africa/lastinta.txt.
10. "New Congo in Great Need of Help to Save Endangered Species," *Worldwide Forest/Biodiversity Campaign News,* July 25, 1997, from World Wide Fund for Nature press release, http://forests.org/.
11. "Mountain Gorillas of Mikeno, Zaire: An Explosive Situation," *Gorilla Conservation News,* May 1997, http://www-anthro.ucdavis.edu/features/gcn+.

12. "Curio Shop Owner Goes to Prison," *IPPL News,* Spring 1998, http://www.org/ippl-news.

13. Debra Forthman, Director of Field Conservation, Zoo Atlanta, and editor, *African Primates,* letter to author, October 1998.

14. Quoted in Daniel Botkin and Edward Keller, "African Rainforest Logging Damage Permanent," *Environmental Science,* http://www.wiley.co.uk/college/environet.

15. Craig Sholley, telephone interview with author, April 1998.

Chapter 3: From Subsistence Hunting to the Bushmeat Crisis

16. Angela Meder, "Bushmeat Trade in the Rainforest: Any Progress?" *Gorilla Journal,* June 1997, http://angela.meder@t-online.de.

17. "Stop the Slaughter," *Biosynergy Institute Fact Sheet,* 1998, bushmeat@biosynergy.org.

18. Kelly Stewart, editorial, *Gorilla Conservation News,* May 1996, http://www-anthro.ucdavis.edu/features/gen.

19. Spinney, "Monkey Business."

20. Quoted in Spinney, "Monkey Business."

21. Karl Ammann, "Conservation in Central Africa, Bushmeat Crisis," *Worldwide Forest/Biodiversity Campaign News,* April 2, 1998, http://forests.org/.

22. Quoted in "WSPA Bushmeat Report," *African Primates: The Newsletter of the Africa Section of the IUCN/SSC Primate Specialist Group,* August 1996, p. 31.

23. Gary Strieker, "Gorillas Are Endangered Prey in Central African Forests," *Worldwide Forest/Biodiversity Campaign News,* February 21, 1997, from Cable News Network, http://forests.org/.

24. Quoted in Anthony Rose, "Finding Paradise in a Hunting Camp; Turning Poachers into Protectors," Bushmeat homepage, http://www.biosynergy.org/bushmeat, from *Journal of the Southwestern Anthropological Association,* vol. 38, issue 3, January 1998.

25. Rose, "Finding Paradise in a Hunting Camp."
26. Rose, "Finding Paradise in a Hunting Camp."
27. Quoted in "Stop the Slaughter," *Biosynergy Institute Fact Sheet.*
28. "Ape Alliance Formed to Fight Trade in Gorilla Meat," *News Journal,* February 27, 1998, http://www.h-jcenter.com/98/kb/27/en4.htm.
29. Quoted in Spinney, "Monkey Business."
30. Anthony Rose, e-mail to author, August 1998.

Chapter 4: Gorilla Tourism:
Gorillas Pay Their Own Way

31. Jane and Steuart Dewar, owners of Gorilla Haven, personal interview with author, Morganton, Georgia, March 1998.
32. Sholley, interview.
33. Sholley, interview.
34. Sholley, interview.
35. Stewart, editorial, *Gorilla Conservation News.*
36. Thomas M. Butynski and Jan Kalina, "Close Encounters Between People and Gorillas," *African Primates,* July 1995.
37. Ursula Karlowski and Iris Weiche, "Gorilla Tourism in Uganda," *Gorilla Journal,* December 1997, http://angela.meder@t-online.de.
38. "Mountain Gorilla," African Wildlife Foundation homepage, 1997, awfwash@igc.apc.org.
39. Quoted in "Close Encounter with Gorillas at Bwindi," *Gorilla Journal,* June 1997, http://angela.meder@t-online.de.

Chapter 5: Humans and Gorillas:
Facing an Uncertain Future

40. Forthman, letter to author.
41. Liz Williamson, "Update from the Karisoke Research Center," Rwanda, January 1998.

42. Charles Horton, Curator of Primates, Zoo Atlanta, interview with author, Atlanta, March 1998.

43. Karl Ammann, "Death in the Forest: Logging Business Means Death for Thousands of Gorillas and Chimpanzees," August 1, 1998, Bushmeat homepage, http://www.biosynergy.org/bushmeat.

Glossary

anthropoid: Manlike; a member of the primate suborder Anthropoidea, which includes monkeys, apes, and humans.

biodiversity: The variety of different biological species that make up an ecosystem.

biosynergy: The beneficial interaction of the different species in an ecosystem; for example, plants produce oxygen needed by animals and animals produce carbon dioxide needed by plants, flowers produce nectar to feed bees and some other animals which fertilize the plants by carrying pollen from one to the next.

blackback: A young male gorilla that has not developed the silvery saddle characteristic of older males.

bonobo: One of the great apes; bonobos were once called pygmy chimpanzees, but in 1929 were formally identified as a separate species; they have smaller heads and more slender, graceful bodies than chimpanzees; their lifestyle is similar to chimps', but they spend more time in the trees and the females play a dominant role in their social structure.

chimpanzee: One of the four great apes; chimpanzees are highly intelligent animals with a very complex social structure; they work in groups to hunt meat for food and sometimes wage war on other chimp groups.

ecosystem: A community of interrelated plants, animals, and bacteria.

ecotourism: Enlightening, participatory travel to environments, both natural and cultural, that ensures the sustainable use, at an appropriate level, of environmental resources while producing economic benefits for the host communities.

feeding ecology: The study of the feeding habits of animals and the effect on their environment and lifestyle.

genetic diversity: The number of unrelated individuals that make up a breeding community.

gestation: Carrying a developing fetus in the uterus from conception to birth; the gestation period for gorillas is about eight and a half months.

habitat: The place and type of environment where a particular type of plant or animal is normally found.

habituate: To make used to, to familiarize; the term used to describe the process of making gorillas accustomed to having humans nearby.

mammal: A warm-blooded vertebrate (an animal with a backbone) that gives birth to live young and nurses its young with milk produced by mammary glands; primates are mammals.

orangutan: One of the four great ape species; the orangutan, a native of Asia, is the only one of the great apes not found in Africa.

poacher: One who illegally hunts protected animals.

primate: A mammal of the order Primata; primates have flexible hands and feet with five digits; primates include humans, apes, monkeys, and lemurs, among others.

prosimian: A primitive primate; its bone structure resembles advanced primates, but its brain, hands, and feet are less highly developed.

rainforest: A dense evergreen tropical forest; **primary rainforest** has never been cut or burned; **secondary rainforest** has been cut or burned and its plant and animal forms are different and will never return to the primary state.

silverback: An adult male gorilla, so called because of the saddle-shaped section of hair on his back that turns silver with age; the dominant figure in a gorilla family.

subsistence hunting: Hunting to feed one's own family or village, not as a commercial venture to produce income.

sustainable use: Using and replacing natural resources so as to prevent their depletion.

synergy: Working together; combined or cooperative action or work.

Organizations
to Contact

African Wildlife Foundation (AWF)
1400 16th St. NW
Suite 120
Washington, DC 20036
(202) 939-3333
e-mail: awfwash@igc.apc.org

The African Wildlife Foundation has been working with the people of Africa to protect their invaluable natural resources since 1961. Most of the staff is based in Africa, working with park managers and communities to safeguard wildlife and wilderness areas. AWF seeks long-term strategies for conserving Africa's natural treasures.

Dian Fossey Gorilla Fund
800 Cherokee Ave. SE
Atlanta, GA 30315-9984
website: http://www.gorillafund.org/

The Dian Fossey Gorilla Fund is dedicated to the conservation and protection of the mountain gorilla and its habitat throughout its range.

Gorilla Foundation
PO Box 620-640
Woodside, CA 94062
website: http://www.gorilla.org/

The Gorilla Foundation promotes the protection, preservation, and propagation of gorillas. Project Koko, a primary focus of the Gorilla Foundation, involves teaching a modified form of American Sign Language to two lowland gorillas, Koko and Michael. The Gorilla Foundation is developing a unique preserve for gorillas on the island of Maui, Hawaii.

IUCN
The World Conservation Union
IUCN/US
Suite 502
1400 16th St. NW
Washington, DC 20036
(202) 797-5454
e-mail: postmaster@iucnus.org

IUCN is one of the world's oldest conservation organizations. It was established in France in 1948 as the "International Union for the Protection of Nature." Today it is a union of other organizations, bringing together 74 governments, 105 government agencies, and 700 non-governmental organizations working at the field and policy levels, together with scientists and experts, to protect nature. Altogether the members of IUCN make up a global network toward the common goal of nature conservation. IUCN promotes the importance of people-oriented conservation and the sustainable use of resources. They compile the Red List of Threatened Species and publish them as *The IUCN Red Data Book.*

Morris Animal Foundation
45 Inverness Dr. East
Englewood, CO 80112
(800) 243-2345
website: http://www.MorrisAnimalFoundation.org

The Morris Animal Foundation funds the Mountain Gorilla Veterinary Center (MGVC), Rwanda. Since 1996 this foundation has monitored the health of wild gorillas and administered emergency medical care when necessary. It is one of the few conservation programs to provide health care and treatment to an endangered species in its natural habitat.

Wildlife Conservation Society (New York Zoological Society)

64th St. and 5th Ave.
New York, NY 10021
(212) 861-6030
website: http://www.centralpark.org

The Wildlife Conservation Society, founded as the New York Zoological Society, has been involved in wildlife and habitat conservation since its inception in 1895.

World Wildlife Fund (WWF)

WWF International
Avenue du Mont-Blanc
CH-1196, Gland
Switzerland
+41 22 364 91 11
website: http://www.panda.org/wwf

WWF is dedicated to protecting the world's wildlife and wildlands. The largest privately supported international conservation organization in the world, WWF has sponsored more than two thousand projects in 116 countries and has more than 1 million members in the United States alone. WWF directs its conservation efforts toward three global goals: protecting endangered spaces, saving endangered species, and addressing global threats.

Suggestions for Further Reading

Tess Lemmon, *Apes.* New York: Ticknor and Fields, 1993. This book, illustrated by John Butler, tells about the characteristics of lesser and great apes. It describes their lives and habits and tells how they are alike and how they differ.

Michael Nichols, *The Great Apes: Between Two Worlds.* Washington, DC: National Geographic Society, 1993. This beautiful book is illustrated with stunning photos by Michael Nichols. It examines all aspects of the great apes and the problems facing them. Contributors include Jane Goodall, George Schaller, and Mary Smith.

Michael Nichols and George B. Schaller, *Gorilla: Struggle for Survival in the Virungas.* New York: Aperture Foundation, 1989. This photographic essay with text by George Schaller and photos by Michael Nichols is beautifully written and illustrated with stunning photographs. Well worth a read even for the layman with limited interest in the subject.

Ian Redmond, *Gorilla.* New York: Knopf, 1995. Despite the title, this excellent book is about all primates. Author Ian Redmond has been active as a gorilla researcher and conservationist since he worked with Dian Fossey in the early days of her landmark study. The book is beautifully illustrated with a combination of photographs and line drawings.

Lois Warburton, *Rainforests.* San Diego: Lucent Books, 1990. Although this book does not specifically relate to

gorillas, it provides a comprehensive overview of the
rainforest. Understanding the rainforest is essential
to understanding conservation issues related to gorilla
habitat.

John Bonnett Wexo, *The Apes.* San Diego: Wildlife Education, 1981. This pamphlet is one of a series of Zoo Books
published by Wildlife Education. It is out of date, but
the basic information is still good. It is well written and
beautifully illustrated. If a library copy can be found
it is well worth a read.

Works Consulted

Books

Elizabeth L. Bennett, Phyllis C. Lee, and Jane Thornback, *Threatened Primates of Africa: The IUCN Red Data Book.* New York: IUCN, 1988. The Red Data Books provide an inventory of threatened species and focus attention on the earth's vanishing wildlife. Basic biological and social structure information is also provided on each species.

Dian Fossey, *Gorillas in the Mist.* Boston: Houghton Mifflin, 1983. An interesting, often entertaining book about Fossey's years studying gorillas in Uganda and Rwanda. It contains some technical information, but is a very readable story about gorilla life and the life of a lone American woman in the jungles of Africa.

John A. Hoyt, *How "Sustainable Use" Is Wiping Out the World's Wildlife.* Garden City Park, NY: Avery, 1994. An opposing argument to the sustainable use theory. The author believes that attempts to manage wildlife through sustainable use always leads to corruption and abuse.

Jeffrey M. Masson and Susan McCarthy, *When Elephants Weep.* New York: Delacorte, 1995. An interesting book supporting the theory that all animals have and express emotions. It provides some insights into the emotions of gorillas and other animals, and points out the changing attitudes among scientists in regard to anthropomorphism.

Robert M. McClung, *Last of the Wild: Vanished and Vanishing Giants of the Animal World.* North Haven, CT: Linnet Books, 1997. An interesting and well-written account of large animal species that are endangered or have already become extinct. The large number of African species that have become extinct in the twentieth century is particularly thought-provoking.

John Nichol, *The Mighty Rainforest.* London: David and Charles, 1990. An interesting and informative book about the rainforests of the world. Beautifully illustrated with many excellent photographs.

George B. Schaller, *The Mountain Gorilla.* Chicago: University of Chicago Press, 1963. A detailed account of a study by Schaller, his wife, and J. T. Emlen, this is the first comprehensive study of free-living gorillas. Photographs in the book were the first ever of gorillas living undisturbed in their natural habitat.

Periodicals, Electronic Sources, and Personal Communication

Karl Ammann, "Conservation in Central Africa, Bushmeat Crisis," *Worldwide Forest/Biodiversity Campaign News,* April 2, 1998, http://forests.org/.

————, "Death in the Forest: Logging Business Means Death for Thousands of Gorillas and Chimpanzees," August 1, 1998, Bushmeat homepage, http://www.biosynergy.org/bushmeat.

Daniel Botkin and Edward Keller, "African Rainforest Logging Damage Permanent," *Environmental Science,* http://www.wiley.co.uk/college/environet.

Thomas M. Butynski and Jan Kalina, "Close Encounters Between People and Gorillas," *African Primates,* July 1995.

John and Margaret Cooper, "Mountain Gorillas—a 1995 Update," *African Primates: The Newsletter of the Africa Section of the IUCN/SSC Primate Specialist Group.* Atlanta, GA: Zoo Atlanta, August 1996.

"Curio Shop Owner Goes to Prison," *IPPL News,* Spring 1998, http://www.ippl.org/ippl-news.

Jane and Steuart Dewar, owners of Gorilla Haven, personal interview with author, Morganton, Georgia, March 1998.

Digit News: The Dian Fossey Gorilla Fund International Newsletter, Summer 1996 and Spring 1997.

"Eco-Warrior Battling to Keep Gabon Rainforest Safe," *Worldwide Forest/Biodiversity Campaign News,* April 8, 1997, from Cable News Network, http://forests.org/.

Manoah Esipisu, "Conservationists Urge World to Help Protect Gorillas," *Worldwide Forest/Biodiversity Campaign News,* December 14, 1997, from Reuters, http://forests.org/.

Debra Forthman, Director of Field Conservation, Zoo Atlanta, and editor, *African Primates,* letter to author, October 1998.

"Four Mountain Gorillas Killed: Reports from the Democratic Republic of Congo Bring Sad News," African Wildlife Foundation press release, June 1997, http://www.awf.org/news.

Howard W. French, "An African Forest Harbors Vast Wealth and Peril," *Worldwide Forest/Biodiversity Campaign News,* April 4, 1996, from *The New York Times,* http://forests.lic. wisc.edu/gopher/africa/lastinta.txt.

"A Global Conservation Strategy for Zoos," *African Primates: The Newsletter of the Africa Section of the IUCN/SSC Primate Specialist Group.* Atlanta, GA: Zoo Atlanta, July 1995.

Charles Horton, Curator of Primates, Zoo Atlanta, interview with author, Atlanta, March 1998.

Ursula Karlowski and Iris Weiche, "Gorilla Tourism in Uganda," *Gorilla Journal,* December 1997, http://angela. meder@t-online.de.

Sally Lahm, "Gabon's Village Hunting: Assessing Its Impact," *African Primates: The Newsletter of the Africa Section of the IUCN/SSC Primate Specialist Group.* Atlanta, GA: Zoo Atlanta, August 1996.

Annette Lanjouw, "International Gorilla Conservation Program (IGCP)," *Gorilla Conservation News,* 1997, http://anthro.ucdavis.edu/gcn//g12igcp.htm.

Eugene Linden, "A Curious Kinship—Apes and Humans," *National Geographic,* March 1992.

Liz Macfie, "Gorilla Tourism in Uganda," *Gorilla Journal,* December 1997.

Angela Meder, "Bushmeat Trade in the Rainforest: Any Progress?" *Gorilla Journal,* June 1997, http://angela.meder @t-online.de.

———, "Certification Withdrawn," *Gorilla Journal,* December 1997, http://angela.meder@t-online.de.

"Mountain Gorilla," African Wildlife Foundation homepage, 1997, awfwash@igc.apc.org.

"Mountain Gorillas of Mikeno, Zaire: An Explosive Situation," *Gorilla Conservation News,* May 1997, http://www-anthro.ucdavis.edu/features/gcn+.

"New Congo in Great Need of Help to Save Endangered Species," *Worldwide Forest/Biodiversity Campaign News,* July 25, 1997, from World Wide Fund for Nature press release, http://forests.org/.

Francine Patterson, "The Case for the Personhood of Gorillas," Gorilla Foundation, http://www.gorilla.org/.

Andrew Purvis/Bukima, "Sounds of Gunfire in the Mist," *Time,* October 2, 1995.

"Rare Mountain Gorillas Die in New Congo Fighting," *Worldwide Forest/Biodiversity Campaign News,* June 10, 1997, from Reuters, http://forests.org/.

Anthony L. Rose, "The African Forest Bushmeat Crisis: Report to the ASP," *African Primates: The Newsletter of the Africa Section of the IUCN/SSC Primate Specialist Group,* Atlanta, GA: Zoo Atlanta, August 1996.

———, "Conservation Becomes a Global Social Movement in the Era of Bushmeat and Primate Kinship." Paper presented to Great Apes of the World Conference, July 1998, Kuching, Sarawok, Malaysia, http:/www.biosynergy.org/bushmeat/papers.htm.

————, e-mail to author, August 1998.

————, "Finding Paradise in a Hunting Camp; Turning Poachers to Protectors," *Gorilla Journal,* Bushmeat homepage, http://www.biosynergy.org/bushmeat, from *Journal of the Southwestern Anthropological Association,* vol. 38, issue 3, January 1998.

Paul F. Salopek, "Gorillas and Humans: An Uneasy Truce," *National Geographic,* October 1995.

Stephen Sautner, "Uganda Has a New Census for Mountain Gorillas," *Worldwide Forest/Biodiversity Campaign News,* December 8, 1997, from World Wildlife Conservation Society, http://forests.org/.

George B. Schaller, "Gentle Gorillas, Turbulent Times," *National Geographic,* October 1995.

Craig Sholley, telephone interview with author, April 1998.

Vir Singh, "Endangered Gorillas in Africa," Animal Rights Resource Site, http://arrs.envirolink.org/.

Laura Spinney, "Monkey Business," *New Scientist,* May 2, 1998, http://www.newscientist.com.

Kelly Stewart, editorial, *Gorilla Conservation News,* May 1996, http://www.anthro.ucdavis.edu/features/gen.

"Stop the Slaughter," *Biosynergy Institute Fact Sheet,* 1998, bushmeat@biosynergy.org.

Gary Strieker, "Baby Gorilla Sales Point to Larger Conservation Issue," *Worldwide Forest/Biodiversity Campaign News,* April 1, 1997, from Cable News Network, http://forests.org/.

————, "Gorillas Are Endangered Prey in Central African Forests," *Worldwide Forest/Biodiversity Campaign News,* February 21, 1997, from Cable News Network, http://forests.org/.

"Urgent Action Needed to Save Congo's Ecosystem," *Worldwide Forest/Biodiversity Campaign News,* August 2, 1997, from Reuters, http://forests.org/.

Liz Williamson, Director, Karisoke Research Center, e-mail message to Dian Fossey Fund staff, Atlanta, 1998.

————, "Update from the Karisoke Research Center," Rwanda, January 1998.

"WSPA Bushmeat Report," *African Primates: The Newsletter of the Africa Section of the IUCN/SSC Primate Specialist Group,* August 1996.

Index

Picture Credits

About the Author

Anne Ake edited an arts magazine for eight years, and with her daughter owned and published *Cool KidStuff,* a children's magazine. She has published articles on varied topics from the arts to nature. She currently edits and designs a newsletter for the state parks of northwest Florida. As a freelance computer graphic and desktop publishing specialist she designs brochure and page layouts. She edited and wrote the text for *Dean Mitchell: The Early Years,* a profile of the American realist painter. As marketing manager of the quality-of-life division of a navy base, Ms. Ake publicizes and produces publications for the installation's leisure and recreational activities.